Effective Teamwork

To Nikolaos Vlissides, for teaching me that emotional wisdom is at the heart of successful cooperation

Effective Teamwork

Practical Lessons from
Organizational Research

Second Edition

Michael A. West

BPS Blackwell

THE BRITISH PSYCHOLOGICAL SOCIETY
St Andrews House, 48 Princess Road East, Leicester LE1 7DR

BLACKWELL PUBLISHING
350 Main Street, Malden, MA 02148-5020, USA
9600 Garsington Road, Oxford OX4 2DQ, UK
550 Swanston Street, Carlton, Victoria 3053, Australia

First edition published 1994 by BPS Books
Second edition published 2004 by The British Psychological Society and Blackwell Publishing Ltd
3 2005

Library of Congress Cataloging-in-Publication Data

West, Michael A., 1951–
  Effective teamwork : practical lessons from organizational research / Michael A. West. — 2nd ed.
      p. cm.
Includes bibliographical references and index.
  ISBN 1-4051-1058-9 (hbk : alk. paper) — ISBN 1-4051-1057-0 (pbk : alk. paper)
  1. Teams in the workplace. I. Title.

  HD66.W473   2004
  658.4'02—dc22

                                                           2003017272

  ISBN-13: 978-1-4051-1058-7 (hbk); ISBN-13: 978-1-4051-1057-0 (pbk)

A catalogue record for this title is available from the British Library.

Set in 10/12½ Meridien
by Graphicraft Ltd, Hong Kong
Printed and bound in the United Kingdom
by TJ International, Padstow, Cornwall

For further information on Blackwell Publishing, visit our website:
www.blackwellpublishing.com

Contents

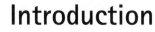

Introduction

At the basis of human society, of the family, and of all social functioning, is the question of how people can combine their efforts and imaginations to work in ways that enhance the quality of life through the achievement of their shared goals. The major challenges that face our species today require answers to the question: how can we interact and cooperate effectively in order to maximize the quality of life for all people while, at the same time, sustaining the resources offered by the planet?

This book does not offer a simple list of solutions to the problems of working together and interacting effectively since there is no easy way of creating effective teams. The world in which we live changes too rapidly for any single set of prescriptions to be adequate. Change is endemic and this demands flexible individuals, flexible teams, and flexible organizations, if they are to be effective and survive.

What this book does suggest is that teams, like individuals, must wisely use the unique and immensely powerful capacities humans possess. We have consciousness and we can manipulate it to learn. What we are able to do – and no other animal can – is to reflect upon our experiences and consciously adapt what we do to meet our changing circumstances. And we can use this ability to learn to dance the dance of teamwork ever more effectively rather than relying on simplistic tips that fail to work in the wide variety of situations faced by teams at work.

This approach to teamwork requires:

- a constant review of the objectives of the team's work;
- intelligent scanning of the environment;
- awareness of the functioning of the team;
- creativity, flexibility, and readiness to change;
- tolerance of ambiguity and difference within the team;
- a preparedness to accept uncertainty as change occurs.

One reason why simple prescriptions cannot be offered for effective team work is that teams operate in varied organizational settings – as diverse as multinational oil companies, voluntary organizations, health care organizations, and the military. The people who constitute these teams are also likely to differ dramatically in personality and background. Within organizations too, teams differ markedly. Increasingly teams are made up of people who have different cultural backgrounds. In some organizations, teams may span national boundaries, including perhaps members located in a number of different nation states, all of whom are required to work effectively together. Moreover, changes in work patterns such as part-time, flexitime, contract, and home working all add further mixes to the heterogeneity of teams. As teams become more diverse in their constitution and functioning, team members must learn to reflect upon, and intelligently adapt to, their constantly changing circumstances in order to be effective. This is the simple message of this book for those who wish to develop effective team functioning.

◆ Task and Social Elements of Team Functioning

There are two fundamental dimensions of team functioning: the task the team is required to carry out, and the social factors that influence how members experience the team as a social unit. The basic reason for the creation of teams in work organizations is the expectation that they will carry out tasks more effectively than individuals and so further organizational objectives overall. Consideration of the content of the task, and the strategies and processes employed by team members to carry out that task, is important for understanding how to work in teams. At the same time, teams are composed of people who have a variety of emotional, social and other human needs that the team as a whole can either help to meet or frustrate.

In order to function effectively, team members must actively focus upon their objectives, regularly reviewing ways of achieving them and the team's methods of working – "task reflexivity." At the same time, in order to promote the well-being of its members, the team must reflect upon the ways in which it provides support to members, how conflicts are resolved and what is the overall social climate of the team – or its "social reflexivity." The purpose of these reviews should be to provide active steps to change the team's objectives, ways of working, or social functioning, in order to promote effectiveness.

**High task
reflexivity**

Type D: Cold efficiency team
High task effectiveness
Average or poor mental health
Short term viability

Type A: Fully functioning team
High task effectiveness
Good mental health
Long-term viability

Low social reflexivity

High social reflexivity

Type C: Dysfunctional team
Poor task effectiveness
Poor mental health
Very low team viability

Type B: Cosy team
Poor task effectiveness
Average mental health
Short-term viability

**Low task
reflexivity**

Figure I.1   Four types of teams and their outcomes

But what does "team effectiveness" mean? We can see team effectiveness as having three main components:

1   *Task effectiveness* is the extent to which the team is successful in achieving its task-related objectives.
2   *Team member well-being* refers to the mental health (e.g., stress levels), growth, and development of team members.
3   *Team viability* is the likelihood that a team will continue to work together and function effectively.

In addition, teams should be assessed in relation to their innovation (the introduction of new and improved products and services) and the level of interteam cooperation. We will return to these two aspects of team effectiveness later in this book but for present purposes we focus on task effectiveness, team member well-being, and team viability.

Figure I.1 shows the two elements of teams, the task and social element, drawn together to illustrate four extreme types of team functioning and the likely effects upon the three principal outcomes of team functioning: task effectiveness, team members' mental health, and team viability.

Type A, the *fully functioning team*, represents a team which is high in both task and social reflexivity, that is, the extent to which the team reflects on and modifies its objectives, processes, task and social support strategies appropriately in changing circumstances. Such teams are likely to have good levels of mental health among team members, high task effectiveness, innovativeness, and sustained viability, that is, they are likely to be able to and want to continue to work together over time.

Type B, the *cosy team*, is high in social reflexivity and low in task reflexivity. This is a team where there is a good deal of warmth, support, and cohesion among team members, but where the ability to get the task done effectively is low. Therefore, while the mental health of team members is good and people feel positively toward the team, the organization's satisfaction with team performance is low. As a result its viability is threatened, although team members wish to continue to work together over a period of time. In the longer term team members' well-being will be adversely affected by the low levels of competence experienced by team members in a team which is minimally task-effective. We like to be successful and effective in our work. Staying in a poorly functioning team will corrode job satisfaction.

Type C, the *dysfunctional team*, is the worst scenario – a team that is low on both task and social reflexivity. Such teams have low viability since team members are dissatisfied with both interpersonal relationships and with the sense of achievement and quality of work.

Finally team type D, the *cold efficiency team*, is a team in which task reflexivity is high, but where the social functioning of the team is poor. Task performance is generally good, but poor social functioning damages team viability and the mental health of members. Team members do not wish to stay working in a team that they perceive as providing little social support and which has a poor social climate. Moreover, because the team does not feel safe, levels of innovation are low.

These two aspects of team functioning, task and social reflexivity, have a direct impact upon the three principal outcomes of team functioning – task effectiveness, team members' mental health, and team viability. In this book we shall examine these elements of team functioning and describe practical ways in which team reflexivity can be enhanced. There are many books available to advise readers about how to work effectively in work teams but this book is different in one key respect. Research evidence drives the content. We will challenge the many assumptions about teamwork that the research evidence does not support. The book describes what research reveals about effective teamwork, not what consultants and pundits guess will work. I also offer examples from my experience of working with many hundreds of teams in a wide variety of settings and across many different countries.[1]

---

[1] If you have additional information about what leads to effective teamwork that you would like to share and that is not covered in this book, or there are areas that you need further information about, email me: m.a.west@aston.ac.uk

Throughout the book, we will focus on how to answer the question "what makes teams effective?" in a way that will prove practically useful to you in working in teams and help you develop them into the fully functioning team that is high in both task and social reflexivity.

Exercise I.1: The Team Reflexivity Questionnaire

How effectively does your team function?

To measure levels of task and social reflexivity in your team, ask all your team colleagues to complete this questionnaire without consulting each other about the answers. Add the scores for task reflexivity and social reflexivity separately, i.e., add all team members' scores for the task element and then all team members' scores for the social element. Divide both totals by the number of people completing the questionnaire. At the bottom of this box are values against which you can determine whether your team's scores are high, low, or average compared with the scores of other teams.

Instructions for completion:

Indicate how far each statement is an accurate or inaccurate description of your team by writing a number in the box beside each statement, based on the following scale of 1 to 7:

Very inaccurate						**Very accurate**
1	**2**	**3**	**4**	**5**	**6**	**7**

(a) **Task reflexivity**
1. The team often reviews its objectives. ☐
2. We regularly discuss whether the team is working effectively together. ☐
3. The methods used by the team to get the job done are often discussed. ☐
4. In this team we modify our objectives in light of changing circumstances. ☐
5. Team strategies are often changed. ☐
6. How well we communicate information is often discussed. ☐

Exercise I.1: (*cont'd*)

7 This team often reviews its approach to getting the job done. ☐

8 The way decisions are made in this team is often reviewed. ☐

Total score ☐

(b) **Social reflexivity**

1 Team members provide each other with support when times are difficult ☐

2 When things at work are stressful the team is very supportive ☐

3 Conflict does not linger in this team. ☐

4 People in this team often teach each other new skills. ☐

5 When things at work are stressful, we pull together as a team. ☐

6 Team members are always friendly. ☐

7 Conflicts are constructively dealt with in this team. ☐

8 People in this team are quick to resolve arguments. ☐

Total score ☐

High scores   42–56

Average scores   34–41

Low scores   0–33

◆ chapter one

Do Teams Work?

There is no hope for creating a better world without a deeper scientific insight in the function of leadership and culture, and of other essentials of group life.

Lewin, 1951, p. 169

key learning points:

- The organizational benefits of team working
- The drawbacks of working in teams – effort, decision making, and creativity
- Teams defined and types of teams
- Tasks for teams
- How to build an effective team
- How to measure team performance

To live, work, and play in human society is to cooperate with others. We express both our collective identity and our individuality in groups and organizations. We have, throughout our history, lived, loved, raised our young, and worked together in groups (Baumeister & Leary, 1995). Our common experiences of living and working together bind us with each other and with our predecessors. It is precisely because human beings have learned to work cooperatively together that we have made such astonishing progress as a species. By mapping the human genome we have discovered the underlying biochemical processes that make us what we are. And we have explored the beginnings and the outer limits of our universe. These extraordinary accomplishments have been accomplished largely by teams, and by teams of teams. When we work cooperatively we accomplish infinitely more than if we work individually. This is the principle of group synergy – that the contribution of the whole group is greater than the sum of its individual members' contributions.

Today we face new demands that make cooperative work in teams more vital and more challenging. To meet the pressures of the global marketplace, organizations are moving away from rigid hierarchical structures to more organic flexible forms. Teams are developing and marketing products, solving production problems, and creating corporate strategy. Managers are experimenting with participation, high-commitment organizations, self-managing work teams, employee–management cooperation, and gainsharing programs. These innovations all involve the explicit use of teams to accomplish central organizational tasks. The team rather than the individual is increasingly considered the basic building block of organizations.

Teamwork is spilling out across organizational and national boundaries. Many manufacturers form teams with suppliers to boost quality, reduce costs, and assure continuous improvement. International alliances are becoming the accepted way to participate in the global marketplace. American and Japanese automakers and other traditional competitors have developed a wide variety of cooperative strategies. Increasingly, people with different organizational and national loyalties from diverse cultural backgrounds and with unequal status are asked to work together. And teams from commercial organizations are linking with those from universities to develop exciting, useful, and radical innovations (West, Tjosvold, & Smith, 2003). Why are they doing this?

In many areas of human activity and endeavor, research has shown how team working can lead to greater efficiency or effectiveness (Weldon & Weingart, 1994). In hard rock mining the introduction of team goals leads to greater quantity of rocks mined. In work safety studies, the introduction of team goals and training sees an increase in safe work behavior. In my work in a coal mining team, I was struck by the fact that it was the team that managed safety by exerting pressure to ensure we all worked in a way that minimized the likelihood of injury. In a study of timber harvesting the introduction of team goals led to a higher output rate; in restaurant services the introduction of team working for staff was associated with higher customer ratings of service quality, comfort, and cleanliness; in an insurance company, increased compliance with a 24-hour reporting standard was found after the introduction of team working; and in truck loading and unloading, truck turnaround time was reduced after the introduction of a team goal (Weldon & Weingart, 1994). Studies in health care have repeatedly shown that better patient care is provided when health professionals work together in multidisciplinary teams (Borrill, West, Shapiro, & Rees, 2000). And the more team working there is in hospitals, the lower the level of patient mortality (West et al., 2002). There is accumulating evidence that when students work in cooperative groups rather than individually, they work harder, help less able group members, and learn more (Slavin, 1983). And not without good reason. It is by working together and pooling our resources (knowledge, abilities, experience, time, money etc.) that we can most effectively accomplish our shared goals.

 ## Why Work in Teams?

Why do people work in teams in modern organizations, and what evidence is there for their value? As organizations have grown in size and become structurally more complex, the need for groups of people to work together in coordinated ways to achieve objectives which contribute to the overall aims of the organization has become increasingly urgent. Trying to coordinate the activities of individuals in large organizations is like building a sandcastle using single grains of sand.

Here are the reasons for implementing team-based working in organizations:

- Teams are the best way to *enact organizational strategy*, because of the need for consistency between rapidly changing organizational environments, strategy, and structure. Team-based organizations, with their flat structures, can respond quickly and effectively in the fast-changing environments most organizations now encounter (Cohen & Bailey, 1997).
- Teams enable organizations to *develop and deliver products and services* quickly and cost effectively. Teams can work faster and more effectively with members working in parallel and interdependently whereas individuals working serially are much slower.
- Teams *enable organizations to learn* (and retain learning) more effectively. When one team member leaves, the learning of the team is not lost. Team members also learn from each other during the course of team working.
- Cross-functional teams promote *improved quality management*. By combining team members' diverse perspectives, decision making is comprehensive because team members question ideas and decisions about how best to provide products and services to

clients. Diversity, properly processed, leads to high quality decision making and innovation (West, 2002).

- Cross-functional design teams can undertake *radical change*. The breadth of perspective offered by cross-functional teams produces the questioning and integration of diverse perspectives that enables teams to challenge basic assumptions and make radical changes to improve their products, services, and ways of working.

- *Time is saved* if activities, formerly performed sequentially by individuals, can be performed concurrently by people working in teams.

- *Innovation is promoted* within team-based organizations because of cross-fertilization of ideas.

- *Flat organizations can be coordinated* and directed more effectively if the functional unit is the team rather than the individual.

- As organizations have grown more complex, so too have their information-processing requirements; *teams can integrate and link* in ways individuals cannot to ensure that information is processed effectively in the complex structures of modern organizations.

- An analysis of the combined results of 131 studies of organizational change found that interventions with the largest *effects upon financial performance* were team development interventions or the creation of autonomous work groups (see Macy & Izumi, 1993).

- *Change is effective* when multiple elements of change are made simultaneously in technology, human resource management systems, and organizational structure, and team working is already present or a component of the change.

- Applebaum and Batt (1994) reviewed 12 large-scale surveys and 185 case studies of managerial practices. They concluded that team-based working led to improvements in organizational performance on measures both of *efficiency and quality*.

- Staff who work in teams report higher levels of *involvement and commitment*, and studies also show that they have *lower stress* levels than those who do not work in teams.

- *Creativity and innovation* are promoted within team-based organizations through the cross-fertilization of ideas (see West, Tjosvold, & Smith, 2003).

Although team working can be effective for all the reasons listed above, it is not the case that the introduction of team working is inevitably successful. Simply relabeling a department in an organization as a "team" does not lead to team working. It may well lead to decreased effectiveness, innovation, and satisfaction. We have to learn the skills of working in teams, yet our educational systems emphasize individual working almost to the exclusion of team working. There are also many barriers to effective team working which team members must learn to overcome or avoid if they are to succeed in achieving synergy – the added advantage of working in teams over and above the outputs from individuals working alone (Brown, 2000). What are these barriers and how can we overcome them?

◆ Barriers to Effective Teamwork

Loss of effort

In the 1890s, French agricultural engineer Max Ringelmann explored whether individuals working alone were more effective than those working in teams. He instructed agricultural students to pull on a rope attached to a dynamometer and measured the amount of pull. Working alone, the average student could pull a weight of 85 kg. Ringelmann then arranged the students in teams of seven and instructed them to pull on the rope as hard as possible. The average pull for a team of seven was 450 kg. The teams were pulling only 75 percent as hard as the aggregated work of seven individuals pulling alone (for more detail see Kravitz & Martin, 1986).

Further research has involved teams solving cognitive problems such as how to transport sheep and wolves safely across a river in a single boat. It showed that although teams took longer than individuals did, overall they were better at achieving correct solutions. Other tasks involved "20 questions" games. Here a particular object is selected and players have to guess what the object is by asking up to 20 questions, to which they are given only a "yes" or "no" answer. Teams were slightly more effective than individuals in getting the correct solution within their 20 questions, but much less efficient in terms of time use. Individuals took, on average, five person minutes to come up with the correct solution. Teams of two took seven person minutes (i.e. 3.5 minutes in real time) and teams of four, 12 person minutes (three minutes in real time). There were no differences between teams of two and four in the likelihood of them getting correct answers (Shaw, 1932).

Why do these effects occur? They result from a phenomenon that psychologists call "social loafing" (Rutte, 2003). Individuals sometimes work less hard when their efforts are combined with those of others than when they are considered individually. Those whose work is difficult to identify and evaluate because of their roles in groups make less effort. This is not to say that all we have to do is single out those who "socially loaf." Rather, it is a characteristic of human behavior that people may work less hard in teams than if they alone were responsible for task outcomes, especially if the task is not intrinsically motivating or they do not feel a strong sense of team cohesion.

The Ringelmann experiments have been replicated by other researchers. In one example, the person at the front of a rope was instructed to pull on the rope and was told that there were six people behind them also pulling. Each person pulling was blindfolded and so was unable to see what was going on behind them. In some cases the other "pullers" simply stood behind the person at the front and made grunting noises suggesting that they were pulling when they were, in reality, making no effort. When individuals *believed* that they were in groups of seven pulling on the rope, they pulled with only 75 percent of the effort they made when they were working individually (Ingham, Levinger, Graves, & Peckham, 1974). In another devious experiment, the researcher instructed individuals to shout as loud as they could, either alone or, as they were told, in groups. They were blindfolded and given ear defenders to cut out visual and sound cues. When people believed they were shouting with others, they exerted only 74 percent of the effort that they made when they believed they were shouting alone, a phenomenon sometimes called "free-riding" (Latané, Williams, & Harkins, 1979). The problem with free-riding is that when it is discovered, the other team members may feel like "suckers" who are being taken advantage of, and they reduce their effort accordingly. Equality of workload in teams therefore affects how much effort team members exert on behalf of the team.

These difficulties present real problems for those working in teams and they challenge the common assumption that "synergy" is produced when individuals work in groups, that is, the idea that groups are more effective than the sum of the contributions of individual members. In such cases 1 + 1 + 1 + 1 + 1 does not necessarily equal five; in many cases 1 + 1 + 1 + 1 + 1 may equal three or even less!

Steiner (1972) proposed that group effectiveness is understandable if we separate out the potential productivity of groups, their actual productivity, and the gap between them. The gap, he asserted, was due to "process losses" such as coordination and communication problems. Below we identify some of the process losses that interfere with team productivity.

Poor problem solving and decision making

The social loafing explanation of poor group performance is helpful in understanding some of the difficulties faced by teams. However, it does not account for the fact that group decision making is sometimes inexplicably flawed. For example, Maier and Solem (1962) presented groups with mathematical questions. They deliberately formed some groups that had an individual in them who knew how to work out the answers. Surprisingly, they found that many of the groups still failed to come up with the correct solutions. Why should this be?

Although we tend to think of groups as somehow reasonable and logical they are greatly influenced by hierarchical considerations. In most primary health care teams, for example, the opinions of the doctors in a meeting will have much greater influence than the opinions of the receptionists. Because of superior status, the doctor exerts more influence over the thinking of the team. Team leaders tend to have more influence over decisions regardless of whether their views are correct or incorrect. Moreover, dominant personalities within groups exert a disproportionate influence over group outcomes. Studies of jury decision making have shown that it may be the person who talks most who has most influence over the jury verdict (McGrath, 1984).

Box 1.1: Baseball or basketball teams?

TEAMWORK IN PRACTICE

In an interesting example of the importance of individual accountability for team work, researchers in the United States attempted to predict the performance of baseball and basketball teams at the end of a season from ratings of the abilities of individual team members. Each team member was given a score from 1 to 10 to denote overall ability within their professional sport. These were then added together and used to predict the eventual performance of a team over a whole season. In one sport the aggregated ratings of the individual abilities of team members predicted team performance with 90 percent accuracy, while in the other sport, they predicted with only 35 percent accuracy.

Which do you think was which?

(The answer to this question is given on page 15 along with an explanation for the finding.)

Overall, research suggests that group decision making in experimental settings is generally superior to that of the average member of the group, but often inferior to that of its most competent individual. In the real world of organizations the situation is rather different but the pitfalls of groups' decision making are not.

Low creativity

Early studies comparing the effectiveness of brainstorming individually or in groups involved creating "statisticized" and "real" groups. Statisticized groups (groups consisting of people who never actually work together, but whose performance is based on the statistical addition of their individual efforts) consisted of five individuals working alone in separate rooms who were given a five-minute period to generate ideas on uses for an object. Their results were aggregated at the end and any redundant ideas due to repetition by different individuals were taken out. Real groups of five individuals worked together for five minutes generating as many ideas as possible and withholding criticism. The statisticized groups produced an average of 68 ideas, while the real groups produced an average of only 37 ideas (Diehl & Stroebe, 1987).

In over 20 studies conducted since 1958, this finding has usually been confirmed. Individuals working alone produce more ideas when they are aggregated than do groups working together. Many managers immediately argue that the quality of ideas produced by groups will be better than the quality of ideas produced by individuals. However, the research does not support this conclusion either. Most measures indicate that individuals working alone produce superior quality ideas (i.e., in numbers of good ideas), and there is no research evidence suggesting that groups produce superior quality. In short, individuals working alone produce a greater quantity of ideas and ideas of at least as good quality as in brainstorming groups (Paulus, 2000).

Why should groups fail to produce the synergistic outcomes that we expect of them in brainstorming groups? The explanation appears to be that when people are speaking in brainstorming groups other individuals are not able to speak and so are less likely to put ideas forward. Moreover, they are busy holding their ideas in their memories, waiting for a chance to speak, and this interferes with their ability to produce other ideas. Furthermore, people may feel inhibited from offering what they see as a relatively ordinary idea after a particularly creative idea has been offered by another group member.

![marker] **Baseball or basketball teams?**

The result (see page 13)

It was possible to predict baseball team scores with 90 percent accuracy since team performance is much more dependent upon individual performance in batting and pitching. Basketball involves passing, coordination, and team strategies for success. Individual accountability is greater in baseball therefore and this makes it easier to predict team performance.

Accepting the fact that production blocking and other factors can inhibit the performance of brainstorming groups, there are three important reasons for working in team settings when proposing new ideas and new ways of doing things. The first is that those who make up teams in "real life" as opposed to laboratory settings, have valuable experience of the particular domains of the team's work. For example, in a primary health care team, there are people with nursing, medical, and social work backgrounds. Together they bring a broad range of important experience to the team's deliberations. It is important that team members are involved in the brainstorming process, so that this wide experience is available as a resource. The second reason for brainstorming in teams is the importance of participation. Involving all those affected by organizational change in the process of change is vital in order to gain commitment and reduce resistance (Heller, Pusić, Strauss, & Wilpert, 1998). Working in brainstorming teams, especially where the teams are focusing on ideas for change, encourages commitment to that process. Finally, many team members argue that it is just more fun to brainstorm in teams, and that humor and laughter are outcomes which themselves can spur creativity.

Notwithstanding these arguments, it is clear from the research that we can alter the mechanics of the process to overcome the production blocking effect. Team members should brainstorm individually to generate their own ideas before bringing them to the team. Then each member should have the opportunity to present all of his or her ideas to the team before evaluation and selection takes place.

Is the picture of less effort, poor decision making, and low creativity as bleak in teams as we have seen it here? An answer to this question emerges from an analysis of 78 studies of individual versus group performance undertaken by Karau and Williams (1993). They found the social loafing effect in 80 percent of the studies but, intriguingly, they found the opposite effect in some. In a small number of studies, group productivity was *greater* than would have been predicted based on knowledge of individual group members' capabilities. This phenomenon, in contrast to "social loafing" is called "social laboring." Instead of experiencing process losses, these groups experienced "process gains." Further analysis reveals that if the team's task is important to them and team members feel the group is significant to them, then the group displays the social laboring effect, demonstrating productivity beyond their calculated potential productivity. Other research suggests that evaluations of the group's performance and the culture of those involved in the research both play a significant role too.

What Karau and Williams's analysis revealed is that most research studies had used trivial team tasks such as clapping, shouting, or finding creative uses for a brick. There was little true teamwork involved since group members did not have to coordinate or build on each other's work. Consequently, participants probably had low task motivation. More complex team tasks that required coordination or integration of members' contributions seemed to produce higher levels of team member motivation and process gains. In one study, teams had simple or complex crossword puzzles to solve. On simple puzzles, there was no difference between the observed and predicted performance of groups based on a knowledge of how well individuals in the groups could do these puzzles. But on the complex puzzles the groups reliably exceeded their predicted performance. Further research showed that the ability of partners in teams may affect performance also and produce process gains. When team members were told they were working with a relatively low ability partner on a brainstorming test (for example), they often worked hard to "make up for" the weaker member. There is evidence too that the less able may raise their performance to a level close to that of the highest performing team member when the discrepancy between their abilities is not too large (Stroebe, Diehl, & Abakoumkin, 1996). One implication for education is that if learning is set up as a cooperative process (with students working together toward a group goal) then a mix of abilities in student groups may raise the level of performance of both the group and of the less able individuals.

The review also showed that in groups with a strong identity, social laboring and process gains were usual. Worchel, Rothgerber, Day, Hart, and Butemeyer (1998) conducted an experiment in which groups had to make paper chains with either another group present or alone. Worchel and colleagues had first checked the facility on the task of the individuals involved so they could predict the potential productivity of the groups. Half of the groups were kitted out with identical colored coats and given a team name to increase the sense of group identity. In this case (strong identity) and in the presence of another competing group, they far exceeded their potential productivity.

The role of culture is also hugely significant, since most of the studies were carried out in the individualistic cultures of the USA and Western Europe. In Eastern cultures, which tend to be more collectivist (people strive more to achieve group rather than their individual goals), the social loafing effect is less marked. Earley (1993) had Israeli (also a collectivist culture) and Chinese trainee managers do an office simulation task in groups and found that they worked harder in groups than they did alone, in contrast to the typical social loafing phenomenon seen in Western research.

It is clear therefore that the motivational value of the team task, the sense of identity in the team, and the national culture can all influence dramatically whether working in teams leads to productivity gains or losses.

 ## The Paradox of Teamwork

So far on this journey into teamwork, we have seen that there is clear evidence of the value of team working for organizational performance, but we have also seen that in relation to the critical areas of effort, decision-making quality, and creativity, teams may be worse than the aggregate of individuals (especially in experimental research) or considerably better. This book offers to explain this paradox and to show how we can harvest the benefits of team work and avoid the drawbacks. To begin to do this we must first understand what we mean by "team," what teams do, and how to build an effective team. It is to these three questions that we now turn.

What is a team?

Many terms describe groups of people working within organizations (e.g., project groups, work groups, quality improvement teams) and the way they work (self-managing, self-directed, self-regulating, semiautonomous, autonomous, self-governing, or empowered teams). This can lead to confusion within organizations when team-based working is being discussed and implemented. So what is a work team? Work teams are groups of people embedded in organizations, performing tasks that contribute to achieving the organization's goals. They share overall work objectives. They have the necessary authority, autonomy, and resources to achieve these objectives.

Their work significantly affects others within or outside the organization. Team members are dependent on each other in the performance of their work to a significant extent; and they are recognized as a group by themselves and by others. They have to work closely, interdependently, and supportively to achieve the team's goals. They have well-defined and unique roles. They are rarely more than 10 members in total (though, as we shall see, size is a big issue in understanding the success and failures of teams). And they are recognized by others in the organization as a team.

What does this mean in practice? First, members of the group have shared objectives in relation to their work. Second, they have genuine autonomy and control so that they can make the necessary decisions about how to achieve their objectives without having to seek permission from senior management. They have both responsibility and accountability. This usually means budgetary control as well. Necessarily, they are dependent upon and must interact with each other in order to achieve those shared objectives. They have an organizational identity as a work group with a defined organizational function (e.g., a primary healthcare team: doctors, nurses, and receptionists). Finally, they are not so large that they would be defined more appropriately as an organization, which has an internal structure of vertical and horizontal relationships characterized by subgroupings. In practice, this is likely to mean that a team is smaller than 15 members (and ideally should be no bigger than six to eight members) and larger than two people.

There are multiple types of teams in organizations:

- *Advice and involvement teams,* e.g., management decision-making committees, quality control (QC) circles, staff involvement groups;
- *Production and service teams,* e.g., assembly teams; maintenance, construction, mining, and commercial airline teams; departmental teams; sales and health-care teams;
- *Project and development teams,* e.g., research teams, new product development teams, software development teams;
- *Action and negotiation teams,* e.g., military combat units, surgical teams, and trade union negotiating teams

Key dimensions on which they differ include:

- degree of permanence – project teams have a defined lifetime that can vary from weeks to years, cockpit "teams" are together for only hours;
- emphasis on skill/competence development – breast cancer care teams must develop their skills over time to a high level, whereas decision-making committees usually have little emphasis on skill development;
- genuine autonomy and influence – manufacturing assembly teams may have little autonomy and influence whereas top management teams are powerful (Flood, MacCurtain, & West, 2001);
- level of task from routine through to strategic – short-haul flights involve crews in routine tasks whereas a government cabinet may be determining penal strategy for a 10-year period.

What do teams do?

The only point of having a team is to get a job done, a task completed, a set of objectives met, whether it is catching a wildebeest for meat, performing surgery on a patient with heart disease, or pushing a large boulder up a hill. Building teams simply to have teams, and without specifying the team task, is like setting the table for guests but not cooking any dinner. It is also likely to damage organizational functioning and encourage conflict, chronic anger, and disruption in the organization.

The tasks that teams perform should be tasks that are best performed by a team. Painting the hull of a super-tanker does not require painters to work interdependently and in close communication over decisions. Each of those involved in the painting simply needs to know which is their section of hull. Navigating the tanker out of a port is likely to require teamwork, as does doing a refit on the engines. Similarly, football and hockey teams are called teams since they have to work interdependently, to communicate constantly, to understand each other's roles, and to collectively implement a strategy in order to achieve their goals (literally).

What tasks are best performed by teams rather than individuals? The following dimensions can be used to analyze the appropriateness of tasks in organizations for teamwork:

Completeness – i.e., whole tasks, not simply putting the studs on the car wheels but assembling the whole transmission system plus wheels.

Varied demands – the task requires a range of skills that are held or best developed by a number of different individuals.

Requirements for interdependence and interaction – the task requires people to work together in interdependent ways, communicating, sharing information, and debating decisions about the best way to do the job.

Task significance – the importance of the task in contributing to organizational goals or to the wider society. A lifeboat team in a rural coastal area with busy shipping lanes, and a health and safety team in a high-risk industry are likely to be highly intrinsically motivated by the significance of their tasks.

Opportunities for learning – providing team members with chances to develop and stretch their skills and knowledge.

Developmental possibilities for the task – the task can be developed to offer more challenges to the team members, requiring them to take on more responsibility and learn new skills over time. The manufacturing team in a factory might develop responsibility for direct interaction with customers over product lead time (the time from ordering to delivery of products) as well as pricing of products.

Autonomy – the amount of freedom teams have over how to do their work, from something as mundane as when to take breaks, through to making decisions about new products or new staff. We will examine the issue of autonomy in depth because it is an area of common failure in the introduction of team working.

Creating teams and then failing to give them the freedom and authority to make the decisions that allow them to accomplish their tasks in the most effective way is a little like teaching someone to ride a bicycle, giving them a fancy road racing bike, and then telling them they can only ride it in their bedroom. Yet in many organizations I see precisely this – teams are created but they are not given the power to make decisions, implement them, and bring about radical change. Moreover, the number of layers in the organizational hierarchy barely changes. Consequently, expectations are not met and team members lose faith in the concept of teamwork other than as a comfortable idea to do with how we can all be supportive to each other. The degree of autonomy of the team reflects the team's influence over:

- the formulation of goals – what and how much it is expected to produce,
- where to work and number of hours (when to work overtime and when to leave),
- choice about further activities beyond the given task,
- selection of production methods,
- internal distribution of task responsibilities within the team,
- membership of the team (who and how many people will work in the team),
- how to carry out individual tasks.

A lifeboat team charged with responsibility for saving people in stricken vessels is likely to rate each of the dimensions (completeness, varied demands, requirements for interdependence, task significance, opportunities for learning, task development, and autonomy) very highly. A group of people responsible for typing the correct zip codes onto wrongly addressed envelopes in the postal service is likely to rate them all very low.

How can we build effective teams?

How can teams at work overcome some of the problems that have been identified so far, such as social loafing and poor decision making or not having an appropriate task? Here are some clear guidelines suggested by research for building an effective team (see Guzzo, 1996; Cohen & Bailey, 1997).

1 *Teams should have intrinsically interesting tasks to perform*
People will work harder if the tasks they are asked to perform are intrinsically interesting, motivating, challenging, and enjoyable. Where people are required to fit the same nut on the same bolt hour after hour, day after day, they are unlikely to be motivated and committed to their work. Where teams have an inherently interesting task to perform there is generally high commitment, higher motivation, and more cooperative working. This therefore calls for very careful design of the objectives and tasks of work teams (see Chapter 2).

2 *Individuals should feel they are important to the fate of the team*
Social loafing effects are most likely to occur when people believe that their contributions to the team are dispensable. For example, in working with primary health care teams, my colleagues and I have

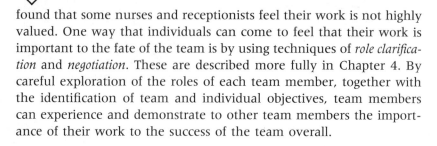
found that some nurses and receptionists feel their work is not highly valued. One way that individuals can come to feel that their work is important to the fate of the team is by using techniques of *role clarification* and *negotiation*. These are described more fully in Chapter 4. By careful exploration of the roles of each team member, together with the identification of team and individual objectives, team members can experience and demonstrate to other team members the importance of their work to the success of the team overall.

3   *Individuals should have intrinsically interesting tasks to perform*
Individual tasks should be meaningful and inherently rewarding. Just as it is important for a team to have an intrinsically interesting task to perform, so too will individuals work harder, be more committed and creative if the tasks they are performing are engaging and challenging. For example, a researcher sitting in on team meetings and observing team processes is more motivated, and has a more creative orientation toward the task, than the researcher who is required to input the data from questionnaires onto a computer.

4   *Individual contributions should be indispensable, unique, and evaluated against a standard*
Research on social loafing indicates that the effect is considerably reduced where people perceive their work to be indispensable to the performance of the team as a whole. Equally important, however, is that individual work should be subject to evaluation. People have to feel that not only is their work indispensable, but also that their performance is *visible* to other members of the team. In laboratory settings, where team members know that the products of their performance will be observed by other members of the team, they are much more likely to maintain effort to the level which they would achieve normally in individual performance. For example, when individuals are told that each team member's shouting will be measured to assess individual contribution to the overall loudness of the team, the classic social loafing effect does not occur. We could measure a doctor's performance by such things as: the number of patients seen; the quality of clinical interactions with patients; patient satisfaction with the general practitioner; the number of home visits completed; the quality of clinical interactions during home visits; prescribing practices; and the quantity and quality of communications with other team members.

5   *There should be clear team goals with in-built performance feedback*
For the same reasons that it is important for individuals to have clear

goals and performance feedback, so too is it important for the team as a whole to have clear team goals with performance feedback. Research evidence shows very consistently that where people are set clear targets to aim at, their performance is generally improved (Locke & Latham, 1991). However, goals can only function as a motivator of team performance if accurate performance feedback is available. For example, in the case of primary health care teams, there should be performance feedback at least annually on all or some of the following indices:

- patient satisfaction with the quality of care given,
- effectiveness of innovations and changes introduced by the team in improving patient care,
- quality of clinical care given in the team,
- improvement in community health,
- the effectiveness with which they have achieved their own objectives as a team,
- quality of team climate and how well team members feel they have worked together,
- quality of intrateam communication,
- quality of relationships with other agencies such as social services, local authority, and hospitals,
- financial effectiveness of the practice,
- efficiency of the practice in reducing patient waiting times,
- improvement in patient access to health care and health promotion.

The more precise the indicators of team performance, the more likely a team is to improve its performance and inhibit the effects of social loafing.

Exercise 1.1: Measuring the effectiveness of your team's performance

1 Identify all those teams or important individuals who have an interest or "stake" in your team's work: These might include
   - management,
   - customers,

Exercise 1.1: (*cont'd*)

- service receivers,
- other teams/departments in your organization,
- those in other organizations,
- the general public,
- you and your team colleagues.

2   Identify the criteria of effectiveness each of these "stakeholders" might use to evaluate your team's effectiveness. Taking those listed under 1 above, these might include:
- meeting the organization's objectives;
- providing quality goods on time and giving good "after sales service";
- providing a helpful, timely, excellent, and considerate service;
- giving useful information;
- cooperating effectively;
- producing goods or services of value to society, in an ethical way;
- having a good quality of working life and experiencing a sense of growth and development.

(These criteria can be made much more detailed for your team and each stakeholder will probably have a number of other criteria.)

3   Give a rating from 1 (*not at all important*) to 7 (*of great importance*) to each criterion. If possible ask other team members to do the same. This can be useful for identifying areas of agreement and disagreement. Customers' criteria should be highly rated.

4   Give a rating from 1 (*not at all effective*) to 7 (*highly effective*) on each criterion in terms of how well you feel the team is achieving on each criterion. Again, if possible, your colleagues should go through a similar rating process. This exercise will give a simple but clear indication of how well you feel the team is achieving in each area. By subtracting the "effectiveness" score from the "importance" score you will also get a good indication of areas where action appears most urgently needed to improve performance. Best of all is to ask the stakeholders themselves to rate the importance and effectiveness of the team's performance on these measures.

◆ Conclusions

The effectiveness of teams is dependent upon a number of psychological factors that can inhibit or improve performance.

- Subtle processes such as social loafing, hierarchical effects, and personality differences can dramatically inhibit team performance.
- Within organizational settings, teams are usually put together and allowed to function without attempts being made to ensure effective functioning.
- The most important elements of team management are specifying individual and team goals and the design of the team task.
- At the same time there must be regular clear and accurate feedback to the team on its performance over time in order to promote team effectiveness.

Team performance is complex and we need practical guidelines based on scientific and applied understanding of team processes to ensure optimum team functioning. These guidelines are to be found in the remaining chapters of this book.

key revision points:

- What are the main benefits of working in teams?

- What are the main drawbacks of working in teams?

- What are the defining characteristics of a team?

- Describe the types of teams in organizations.

- How do they differ?

- Which kinds of tasks are appropriate for teams and which are not?

- How can we build effective teams?

FURTHER READING

Baumeister, R. F. & Leary, M. R. (1995). The need to belong: Desire for interpersonal attachments as a fundamental human motivation. *Psychological Bulletin, 117*, 497–529.

Brown, R. (2000). *Group processes* (2nd edn.). Oxford: Blackwell.

Cohen, S. G. & Bailey, D. E. (1997). What makes teams work? Group effectiveness research from the shop floor to the executive suite. *Journal of Management, 23*, 239–90.

Karau, S. J. & Williams, K. D. (1993). Social loafing: A meta-analytic review and theoretical integration. *Journal of Personality and Social Psychology, 65*, 681–706.

Mohrman, S., Cohen, S., & Mohrman, L. (1995). *Designing team based organizations*. London: Jossey Bass.

West, M. A. (ed.) (1996). *The handbook of work group psychology*. Chichester, UK: Wiley.

West, M. A., Tjosvold, D., & Smith, K. G. (eds.) (2003). *The international handbook of organizational teamwork and cooperative working*. Chichester, UK: Wiley.

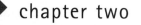

◆ chapter two

Creating Teams

Many times a day I realize how much of my own outer and inner life is built upon the labors of my fellow men, both living and dead, and how earnestly I must exert myself in order to give in return as much as I have received.

Albert Einstein

key learning points:

- The stages of team development

- Ability of team members and team performance

- Personality mixes and teamwork

- Skills for working in teams

- Effects of diversity in functional background on teamwork

- The effects of demographic (age, gender, tenure, and culture) diversity on teamwork

When you play in a great team, it doesn't matter how good the players are individually, it's how well you play together and understand each other's styles and moves. It's really about intuitive ways of playing off each other.

The talent in the team is amazing. Individually they are outstanding but for some reason they just can't make it happen together. I think there are maybe too many prima donnas in the team.

It's about finding the magic mix, that blend of skills and experience that combines maturity, energy, determination, and creativity. It's like a ballet when it happens. Beautiful to behold!

These quotations from players in sports teams could come as easily from members of work teams and they show we must think carefully about how we create teams. Typically, individuals are recruited and selected to work as part of a group because they have the technical skills and experience necessary for particular aspects of the job. For a top management team in a manufacturing organization, directors look to appoint managers for production, human resource management, finance, R&D, and marketing, and to appoint people with outstanding skills in these areas. This is, of course, entirely reasonable. Also reasonable, however, would be an examination of the degree to which candidates have the personal characteristics necessary to work effectively as part of a team. Since it is unlikely that all are equally well suited to team work, personal characteristics and preferences should be considered in the recruitment of team members. But it does not stop there, since there are specific skills of team working just as there are skills associated with any complex behavior; do candidates have the skills to work in a team and are they good at using them? The third quotation indicates we also need to ponder on the mix of people in the team. If we have a team of talented, creative, temperamental individualists working together on a problem, the team will probably fail. Or, if the team is made up of dominant leaders, hostility is likely to be the main team outcome.

The context of work teams dictates consideration of diversity, including visible attributes such as gender and age, as well as less obvious aspects of diversity such as values, skill, social status, background, education, and (hugely important in our multicultural world) societal culture. How do we make judgments about the "magic mix" our interviewee above referred to? And is diversity a good thing in teams or should we be looking to avoid the inevitable process losses diversity produces? We explore these questions in this chapter. Before we do so, we will examine how teams develop over their lifespan, since this helps to provide the context for understanding how to build effective teams. The issues to consider at the outset of a team's life are very different from those during the mature performing stage.

Understanding how to create teams requires us to understand that team processes vary according to the stage of their development and that their beginnings require particular consideration. Like any life form they develop and change, and what is significant at one point in their lives is replaced at other points by new influences. Whether it be humans, plants, or planets, understanding them requires an appreciation of their development.

The Stages of Team Development

The best-known and most widely used model of team development (Tuckman, 1965) suggests five stages: forming, storming, norming, performing, and adjourning.

Forming: there is often considerable anxiety at the forming stage. Team members ask testing questions that reflect their concern about roles – particularly the nature of the leadership role – and about the resources available to the team. Individuals within the team seek out information about other team members, particularly their backgrounds and experience in the type of work that the team will undertake. They are likely to be anxious about external expectations of the team, and to request information about rules and regulations that will affect the team's working methods. At this early stage, team members may be rather guarded in the information they divulge. Their early judgments of one another will therefore be based on limited information. The most important task at this stage is to ensure that team goals are clearly stated and agreed.

Storming: during the storming stage, conflict emerges between individuals and subgroups. The choice, authority, and/or competency of the leader are challenged, and individuals resist attempts by the leader to control team processes. Members question the value and feasibility of the team task. Hidden tensions surface during this stage. Individuals may react strongly and opinions may become polarized. This stage can also see an emerging honesty and openness within the team as they work through the conflicts. The team leader must build positively on this to gain shared commitment to the team goals, to build trust, begin the definition of team roles, and to establish conflict resolution strategies for the team.

Norming: during norming, conflicts are resolved and the team begins to address the task with positive cooperation. Plans are made and work standards are established. Norms or agreed rules and ways of working emerge regarding team and individual behavior. Team members more readily communicate their views and feelings, and networks for mutual support emerge. During this stage the team leader should allow the team to take more responsibility for its own planning and team processes, perhaps allowing team members to make mistakes and encouraging the team to reflect upon them. It is important to ensure that norms are established that meet the needs of the organization, since teams could develop norms that are destructive to effective functioning (e.g., it's acceptable to be late or not to turn up for team meetings).

Performing: team members begin to see successful outcomes as their energies focus constructively on the joint task. They settle into an effective team-working structure, within which individual members feel comfortable, and begin to work together more flexibly. The team leader can usually withdraw from day-to-day involvement, a change that is acknowledged and accepted by team members. At this stage, systems of regular review should be established to ensure that the team continues to be effective and responsive to its environment.

Adjourning: not all teams go through the final adjourning stage as a team, but at various times of its life key members will leave or major projects will be completed or curtailed. It is important that the effects of such changes on the life of the team should be acknowledged: teams may revert to earlier stages of development depending on their levels of maturity, their stability, and the scale of the change.

Not all teams will fit neatly into Tuckman's sequence of team development. A team might go back and forth, revisiting stages to deal with them gradually at different levels. Team leaders can encourage teams by introducing an effective team-development process and ensuring that the team task is clear, that conflicts are processed with satisfactory (and ideally creative) consequences, that team members' roles are clear, that positive norms are established, that the team performs well, and that it disbands constructively and in a timely fashion when its task is complete.

But the first issue to address is how to select the right team members and with the right mix. These two questions will occupy the rest of this chapter. We begin by exploring ability and personality, skills of teamwork, skill diversity, and finally demographic diversity. This exploration reveals some surprising discoveries.

◆ Personality and Ability

For individual jobs, general mental ability is one of the best predictors of job performance (Schmidt & Hunter, 1998). Not surprisingly, team members' overall ability predicts team performance. This was demonstrated in one study of military crews (Tziner & Eden, 1985) which showed that people of high ability contributed most to performance when all the other crew members were also high in ability. In the last chapter, we pointed to some research that suggests mixed ability teams may perform better than high ability teams on a learning task. Nevertheless, overall the evidence is clear in suggesting that teams composed of members high in ability will perform better than would be predicted by the sum of their abilities (Devine & Phillips, 2000) particularly on unfamiliar tasks.

What of personality? The "Big Five" model of personality (Barrick & Mount, 1991) offers a robust personality model that we can use to analyze mix of personality in teams and the effects on team performance. The model describes five dimensions of personality:

Openness to experience – fantasy, actions, and ideas;
Conscientiousness – competence, order, and self-discipline;
Extroversion – positive emotions, gregariousness, and warmth;
Agreeableness – trust, straightforwardness, and tender-mindedness;
Neuroticism – anxiety, self-consciousness, and vulnerability.

It is not surprising that certain personality dimensions are linked to effective team work, but what is enlightening is the discovery that the particular dimensions that emerge as important depend on the type of task. In interdependent teams where individual contributions to team success are easily recognized and rewarded, hardworking and dependable team members are most successful (Mount, Barrick, & Stewart, 1998). Other team members see these conscientious individuals as valued team members because they can be relied upon to perform their part of the work. Conscientiousness is valuable in team settings because hierarchical control is reduced, so there is a need for self-discipline (Mount et al., 1998; Barrick, Stewart, Neuberg, & Mount, 1998). Such self-discipline is particularly important if team-based rewards are used in the organizations (i.e., compensation is based on performance of the entire team) because team member pay is dependent on the successful performance of each and every team member. Teams composed of conscientious team members perform at a high level, particularly on productivity and planning tasks.

However, teams with high levels of extroversion are better at decision making than at planning and performance tasks, probably because their warmth and optimism helps them in persuading others to accept their decisions. For teams requiring creative decisions or innovation, openness rather than conscientiousness or extroversion are most important. In effect, the research evidence suggests that teams composed of conscientious people with high levels of extroversion are likely to be most effective. Having high levels of agreeableness in

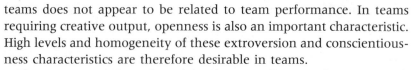
teams does not appear to be related to team performance. In teams requiring creative output, openness is also an important characteristic. High levels and homogeneity of these extroversion and conscientious-ness characteristics are therefore desirable in teams.

There are a number of models of personality mix for team work that are popular in business and it is appropriate to subject them to scrutiny and see how they stand this test. For example, some organ-izations try to achieve compatibility within teams based on the cognitive styles of members by using the Myers–Briggs Type Indicator assessment instrument (a questionnaire measure of cognitive style; Myers & Briggs, 1962). This describes four dimensions: extroversion –introversion, sensing–intuition, thinking–feeling, and judging–perceiving. The first criterion defines the source and direction of energy expression for a person. The extrovert has a source and direction of energy expression mainly in the external world while the introvert has a source of energy mainly in the internal world. The second criterion defines the method of information perception by a person. Sensing people believe mainly information they receive directly from the external world. Intuitive people believe mainly information they receive from the internal or imaginative world. The third criterion defines how people process information. Thinking people make deci-sions mainly based on logic; feeling people make decisions based on emotion. The fourth criterion defines how people implement the information they have processed. Judging people organize their life events and act strictly according to their plans; perceiving people are inclined to improvise and seek alternatives. The different combina-tions of the dimensions describe each person as being of one of 16 types. Much is made of the value of combinations of these types in teams. However, there is little rigorous research evidence presently available showing a relationship between compatibility of Myers–Briggs types and team performance.

Schutz's (1967) theory of fundamental interpersonal relations orientations (FIRO) seeks to explain how personal attributes of team members affect team performance. Schutz sees three basic human needs expressed in group interaction: needs for inclusion, control, and affection. The theory proposes that groups composed of people with compatible needs (e.g., high initiators of control and high receivers of control) will be more effective than groups composed of those with incompatible needs. Compatible groups have a balance of initiators and receivers of control, inclusion, and affection. In an incompatible group, for example, some members may want more affection than others are able to provide. Although some research has shown that compatibility on the dimensions of control and affection predicted time to task completion in teams of managers working in a laboratory setting, there is a good deal of research showing no relationships between compatibility and group performance (e.g., Hill, 1982). Indeed, Hill (1982) found that incompatibility on FIRO-B was associated with higher productivity in teams of systems analysts. Perhaps what this research reveals is that the imperatives of doing the job in teams at work override issues of personal compatibility, and that when we need to get a job done (working in the emergency room of a children's hospital) we adapt to each other's differences and don't let issues of compatibility influence our effectiveness. One message of this book is that if we create the right conditions for team working, good relationships will follow, while the reverse is not necessarily the case (Mullen & Copper, 1994).

Another popular approach to team personality issues is Belbin's Team Roles Model (Belbin, 1993). Belbin suggests that there are nine team personality types and that a balance of these team personality types is required within teams (see Box 2.1). Belbin argues that a balance of all nine team roles is required for a team to perform effectively. Individuals usually incorporate several of these team role types in their personality profiles and so, within teams of only three or four individuals, there may nevertheless be primary and secondary team role types which cover the nine areas of team role functioning. However, there is little evidence to support these predictions and the instruments developed to measure the team role types (Belbin, 1981, 1993) do not appear to have good psychometric properties (Anderson & Sleap, in press; Furnham, Steele, & Pendleton, 1993). Scales have low internal consistencies and very high intercorrelations. It is likely that the Team Roles Inventory taps the "Big Five" measures of personality and thus reflects some of the findings about personality types and team functioning described above. The model, however, is one that many managers and consultants find immensely practical in helping them to think through the dynamics of their teams. Again though, notions of compatibility are not well supported; when we need to catch a wildebeest on the savannah to eat and survive, the issue is probably not how compatible we are but how well we work as a team to deploy our individual hunting skills collectively.

Box 2.1: Belbin's team role theory

Based on research with over 200 teams conducting management business games at the Administrative Staff College, Henley, in the UK, Belbin identified nine team types. Almost always people have a mix of roles and will have dominant and subdominant roles.

Coordinator

The coordinator is a person-oriented leader. This person is trusting, accepting, dominant, and committed to team goals and objectives. The coordinator is a positive thinker who approves of goal attainment, struggle, and effort in others. The coordinator is "someone tolerant enough always to listen to others, but strong enough to reject their advice." The coordinator may not stand out in a team and usually does not have a sharp intellect.

Shaper

The shaper is a task-focused leader, who abounds in nervous energy, has high motivation to achieve, and for whom winning is the name of the game. The shaper is committed to achieving ends and will "shape" others into achieving the aims of the team. He or she will challenge, argue, or disagree and will display aggression in the pursuit of goal achievement. Two or three shapers in a team, according to Belbin, can lead to conflict, aggravation, and in-fighting.

Plant

The plant is a specialist idea maker characterized by high IQ and introversion while also being dominant and original. The plant takes radical approaches to team functioning and problems. Plants are more concerned with major issues than with details. Weaknesses are argumentativeness and a tendency to disregard practical details.

Box 2.1: (cont'd)

TEAMWORK IN PRACTICE

Resource investigator

Resource investigators are people who are never in their rooms, and if they are on the phone. The resource investigator is someone who explores opportunities and develops contacts. Resource investigators are good negotiators who probe others for information and support and pick up other people's ideas and develop them. They are sociable, enthusiastic, and good at liaison work and exploring resources outside the team. Their weaknesses are a tendency to lose interest after initial fascination with an idea, and they are not usually a source of original ideas.

Company worker/implementer

Implementers are aware of external obligations, are disciplined, conscientious, and have a positive self-image. They are tough-minded and practical, trusting and tolerant, respecting established traditions. They are characterized by low anxiety and tend to work for the team in a practical and realistic way. Implementers figure prominently in positions of responsibility in larger organizations. They do the jobs that others do not want to do and do them well, for example, disciplining employees. Implementers are conservative, inflexible, and slow to respond to new possibilities.

Monitor evaluator

According to the model, this is a judicious, prudent, intelligent person with a low need to achieve. Monitor evaluators contribute particularly at times of crucial decision making because they are capable of evaluating competing proposals. The monitor evaluator is not deflected by emotional arguments, is serious-minded, slow in coming to a decision because of a need to think things over, and takes pride in never being wrong. Weaknesses are that they may appear dry and boring or even overcritical. They are not good at inspiring others. Those in high level appointments are often monitor evaluators.

TEAMWORK IN PRACTICE

Box 2.1: (cont'd)

Team worker

Team workers make helpful interventions to avert potential friction and enable difficult characters within the team to use their skills to positive ends. They keep team spirit up and allow other members to contribute effectively. Their diplomatic skills together with their sense of humor are assets to a team. They have skills in listening, coping with awkward people, and being sociable, sensitive, and people-oriented. They are indecisive in moments of crisis and reluctant to do things that might hurt others.

Completer finishers

The completer finishers dot the i's and cross the t's. They give attention to detail, aim to complete, and to do so thoroughly. They make steady effort and are consistent in their work, and are not so interested in the glamor of spectacular success. Weaknesses, according to Belbin, are that they are overanxious and have difficulty letting go and delegating work.

Specialist

The specialist provides knowledge and technical skills that are in rare supply within the team. They are often highly introverted and anxious and are self-starting, dedicated, and committed. Their weaknesses are single-mindedness and a lack of interest in other peoples' subjects.

Teamwork Skills

When we create teams we should think beyond the relatively unchangeable aspects of the person such as their personality and think more of their motivation, knowledge, and skills for working in teams. This includes their preferences for working in teams; whether they have an individualist or collective approach to working with others; their basic social skills such as listening, speaking, and cooperating; and their team working skills such as collaboration, concern for the team, and interpersonal awareness.

Social skills

Social skills include:

- active listening skills – listening to what other people are saying and asking questions);
- communication skills – planning how to communicate effectively taking into account the receiver, the message, and the medium;
- social perceptiveness – being aware of others' reactions and understanding why they react the way they do;
- self-monitoring – being sensitive to the effects of our behavior on others;
- altruism – working to help colleagues;
- warmth and cooperation;
- patience and tolerance – accepting criticism and dealing patiently with frustrations (Peterson et al., 2001).

Such skills are likely to be particularly valuable to the performance of teams and could therefore be among the criteria for selecting team members.

Knowledge, skills, and abilities (KSAs) for teamwork

In teamwork settings, employees need the abilities to perform the job as individuals as well as the abilities to work effectively in a team, because both are important for team performance (West & Allen, 1997). Stevens and Campion (1994, 1999) propose that effective team functioning depends on teamwork abilities, focusing on team members' knowledge of how to perform in teams that extend beyond the requirements for individual job performance. Based on the literature on team functioning, they identified two broad skill areas (interpersonal KSAs and self-management KSAs), consisting of a total of 14 specific KSA requirements for effective teamwork (see Box 2.2). Stevens and Campion (1994) developed a 35-item multiple choice test in which respondents are presented with challenges they may face in the workplace and asked to identify the strategy they would most likely follow. They found that team members' scores on this test were significantly related to team performance in several studies (McDaniel, Morgeson, Finnegan, Campion, & Braverman, 2001).

TEAMWORK IN PRACTICE

Box 2.2: Knowledge, skills and abilities for teamworking

I Interpersonal Team Member KSAs

A Conflict resolution	1 Fostering useful debate, while eliminating dysfunctional conflict
	2 Matching the conflict management strategy to the source and nature of the conflict
	3 Using integrative (win–win) strategies rather than distributive (win–lose) strategies
B Collaborative problem solving	4 Using an appropriate level of participation for any given problem
	5 Avoiding obstacles to team problem solving (e.g., domination by some team members) by structuring how team members interact
C Communication	6 Employing communication that maximizes an open flow
	7 Using an open and supportive style of communication
	8 Using active listening techniques
	9 Paying attention to nonverbal messages
	10 Taking advantage of the interpersonal value found in greeting other team members, engaging in appropriate small talk, etc.

II Self-management Team KSAs

D Goal setting and performance management	11 Setting specific, challenging, and achievable team goals
	12 Monitoring, evaluating, and providing feedback on performance
E Planning and task coordination	13 Coordinating and synchronizing tasks, activities, and information
	14 Establishing fair and balanced roles and workloads among team members

Source: Adapted from Stevens and Campion (1994)

Regardless of their task specialism or their preferred team role, there are certain attributes that all team members need to demonstrate if the team is to achieve its goal. We should create teams of people who have all or most of the KSAs described by Stevens and Campion and train all team members to develop these KSAs.

Exercise 2.1: Knowledge, skills, and abilities for teamwork

Complete the questionnaire below to assess your own KSAs for teamwork.

You should identify areas where your teamwork performance is not adequate (when you indicate "very little") and aim to improve your KSAs in these areas. A better measure is to ask your team colleagues to rate you (or all members of team) on these dimensions, so you have more objective feedback on your KSAs.

Communication	A great deal	Very little
I understand and use communication networks, making sufficient contact with colleagues	☐	☐
I communicate openly and supportively	☐	☐
I listen actively and nonevaluatively	☐	☐
There is a consistency between my verbal and nonverbal behavior	☐	☐
I value and offer warm greetings and small talk with colleagues	☐	☐

Goal setting and performance management		
I help establish clear and challenging team goals	☐	☐
I monitor and give supportive feedback on team and individual performance	☐	☐

Exercise 2.1: (*cont'd*)

	A great deal	Very little
Planning and coordination		
I help to coordinate activities, information, and working together between members	☐	☐
I help to clarify tasks and roles of team members and ensure balance of workloads	☐	☐
I respond positively and flexibly to feedback from team members	☐	☐
Collaborative problem solving		
I identify problems requiring participation of all team members in decision making	☐	☐
I use appropriate ways of involving team members in decision making	☐	☐
I explore and support proposals for innovation in the team	☐	☐
Conflict resolution		
I discourage undesirable conflict	☐	☐
I employ win–win rather than win–lose negotiation strategies	☐	☐
I recognize types and sources of conflict and implement appropriate conflict resolution and reduction strategies	☐	☐

Diversity of Team Members

How similar to or different from each other should team members be?
If all have very similar backgrounds, views, experiences, and values,
team members are likely to pass through the norming and storming

phases quickly, establish good relationships, and perform their jobs effectively. Where team members are very dissimilar to each other, they are likely to find that early interactions, particularly during norming and storming, are characterized by intense conflict as members try to understand each other and agree on the objectives, leadership, and roles in the team. Over time though, their greater diversity of perspectives will offer a range of views and knowledge, which will in turn produce better decision making, more innovation, and higher levels of effectiveness. But such synergy will be achieved only with a high level of effort to ensure effective integrated team working. In practice, how can we create teams that are appropriately diverse?

One perspective on this comes from the attraction–selection–attrition model (ASA; Schneider, Goldstein, & Smith, 1995), which proposes that teams attract people similar to existing team members, they select such people, and those who are dissimilar are likely to leave the team. Another theory (similarity–attraction theory; Byrne, 1971) proposes that we are attracted to those who are similar to us and thus contrive to organize and evaluate our social worlds accordingly. The tendency of team members and team leaders will therefore be to create homogeneous teams. Is this a helpful tendency in relation to team effectiveness and innovativeness?

In order to answer this question, Susan Jackson (1996) advocates distinguishing between task-related diversity (such as organizational position or specialized technical knowledge), and relations-oriented diversity (such as age, gender, ethnicity, social status, and personality) (see also Maznevski, 1994). She concludes that, in relation to tasks requiring creativity and quality of decision making, "the available evidence supports the conclusion that team task-related diversity is associated with better quality team decision-making" (Jackson, 1996, p. 67; see also Joshi & Jackson, 2003). We examine task-related diversity first.

Task-related diversity

When teams form or when new team members are recruited, leaders and team members strive to appoint people who will have the skills to enable the team to accomplish its task. In the case of an R&D team in pharmaceuticals, the team will need a number of chemists, a marketing specialist, a finance specialist, and probably a specialist in the product area.

Beyond this though, is the question of how much diversity to encourage. Does the team recruit chemists with the skills in the specific product area or do they broaden the range of skills available to the team by bringing in someone with experience from cosmetics as well as medicines, since there may be some valuable cross-fertilization from these apparently unrelated areas? Should we aim to build teams by specifying quite narrowly the range of skills absolutely necessary for the task and bring together people with very similar backgrounds and experience? Or should we specify broadly the range of skills required but hope to attract team members with differing and even unusual skills and experiences?

One narrow approach to answering these questions is "skill mix," defined as the balance between trained and untrained, qualified and unqualified, and supervisory and operative staff within a service area as well as between different staff groups. Optimum skill mix is achieved when the desired standard of service is provided, at the minimum cost that is consistent with the efficient deployment of trained, qualified, and supervisory personnel and the maximization of contributions from all staff members. A skill mix review involves discovering what activities need to be carried out within the team, who is currently doing them, the skill level of people doing them, the minimum level of skill required to do them, and the potential for combining tasks in new ways to create in some cases new roles and staff groupings. This orientation to selecting for teams therefore focuses on the identification of particular technical skills required by the team that are not already supplied, or are supplied at higher cost, by others in the team.

Another approach suggests that diversity should be developed within teams because of effects on innovation. For example, in a study of 100 primary health care teams, Carol Borrill and colleagues (Borrill, West, Shapiro, & Rees, 2000) found that the greater the number of professional groups represented in the team, the higher the levels of innovation in patient care. Groups that contain people with diverse and overlapping knowledge domains and skills are particularly creative (Dunbar, 1997). Wiersema and Bantel (1992) found that strategic management initiatives were more likely to be made by top management teams whose members had a high level of diversity in their educational specialization. The biggest ever study of these issues was undertaken by a UNESCO-sponsored international research group which set out to determine the factors influencing the scientific performance of 1,222 research teams (Andrews, 1979). They assessed diversity in six areas: projects, interdisciplinary orientations, specialties, funding resources, R & D activities, and professional functions. The results showed that diversity and the extent of communication both within and between research teams had strong relationships with scientific recognition of their teams, R & D effectiveness, number of publications, and the applied value of their work. Diversity of functional backgrounds may also influence team performance as a result of the higher level of external communication that team members initiate, precisely because of their functional diversity. Varied links favor innovation through the incorporation of diverse ideas and models gleaned from different functional areas. And research does show that the greater a team's functional diversity, the more team members communicate outside the team's boundaries and the higher their levels of innovation (Ancona & Caldwell, 1992).

All well and good. But diversity also has a down side. When diversity begins to threaten the group's safety and integration, then creativity and innovation implementation will suffer. For example, when diversity reduces group members' agreement about team objectives, teams will fail. The challenge is to create sufficient diversity within the team without threatening their shared view of their task and their ability to communicate and work effectively together. Where diversity is very low, the group pressures will be toward conformity rather than integration. Where diversity is very high, there is unlikely to be adequate agreement in the team about its task, ways of working, and roles; consequently communication and coordination of efforts will be problematic continually. Thus the research team composed of a statistician, a Marxist sociologist, a quantitative organizational psychologist, a social constructionist, and a political scientist may be so diverse that they are unable to develop a coherent and innovative program of research to discover under what circumstances nursing teams on hospital wards acknowledge and discuss medication errors. This is not to suggest that the less diverse a group is, the better integrated and safer it will be for its members. On the contrary, it is likely that members only learn integrating skills and discover safety through the effective management of diversity. Where the group is homogeneous then there will be strong pressures for conformity. Where the group is heterogeneous there will be pressures to manage (via group processes) the centrifugal forces of diversity that could lead to the disintegration of the group and could also threaten individual members (e.g., others' differing perspectives threatening one's own beliefs). We only discover a solid sense of safety through the management of apparently threatening environments. Children who explore their environment are more confident than children who never stray from their mothers.

One resolution to this problem is to suggest that diversity of knowledge and skills will be beneficial for team performance and innovation if, and only if, group processes minimize process losses due to diversity, such as disagreements, misunderstandings, and suspicion arising from diversity of perspectives (West, 2002). Groups composed of people with differing professional backgrounds, knowledge, skills, and abilities, will be more innovative than those whose members are similar, because they bring usefully differing perspectives on issues to the group (Paulus, 2000). Their divergence of views offers multiple perspectives and the potential for constructive debate. Diversity also contributes to the magnitude of the team's total pool of task-related skills, information, and experience. If the differences in information and perspectives are worked through in the interests of effective decision making and task performance, rather than on the basis of motivation to win or prevail, or because of conflicts of interest, this in turn will generate good performance and high levels of innovation (Tjosvold, 1998; Paulus, 2000).

Relations diversity

As I experience the cultures and practices of a variety of organizations, it is remarkable to observe how much they differ in their diversity. Some companies, such as a large construction company I work with, are dominated by white, male, British, 30 to 50 year olds. Others, such as my own business school, has a wide range of employees, with more than 30 percent coming from countries other than those in the United Kingdom, and with a wide range of ages and tenure in the organization and a balance of genders. This leads to great variation in the structure of teams in relation to demographic and other "relations" differences (such as how diverse the team is in time of team membership). What do we know about relations diversity?

Age

In teams composed of people of very different ages, people are more likely to leave than in teams homogeneous with respect to age. Moreover, in top management teams, we found that age-diverse teams ran companies that were subsequently less profitable (West, Patterson, & Dawson, 1999). There is some emerging evidence too that age diversity and team innovation may have a U-shaped relationship: very high or very low diversity in age being associated with low levels of innovation, and moderate diversity being linked to relatively high levels of innovation.

Gender

In our work with teams, I and my colleagues have carefully examined differences between teams with varying gender mixes. The results suggest that the more women there are in a team (excluding women-only teams) the more positively do all team members report the team's functioning. This may be because women focus more on the participation and involvement of their colleagues, whereas men are more likely to focus on the task (Eagly & Johnson, 1990). Moreover, men are more likely to interrupt women in team meetings and to pay less attention to their contributions (West et al., 1998).

Team tenure

In top management teams of manufacturing companies, Malcolm Patterson, Jeremy Dawson, and I found that the longer the teams had been together, the more profitable their companies subsequently were (West, Patterson, & Dawson, 1999). And there is increasing evidence from studies in a variety of sectors in the USA that the longer teams are together, the better they tend to perform (Hackman, 2002). This makes sense, since the longer they work together, the more they come to have a clear understanding of each other's styles of working and strengths. Imagine a football team in which the members were constantly changing. They would not learn to play together effectively, since their learning about each other's styles and techniques would be disrupted constantly. Teams in which the members have very dissimilar tenure not surprisingly report that their teams are less effective.

Culture

We live in a global village where international travel and communication have become the norm. Societies too are increasingly multicultural, and organizations and teams must mirror the diversity in the communities they serve in order that they can understand and respond to the needs of the clients they serve. Does cultural diversity enable or hinder team performance? This is not a simple question to answer but in one of the very few longitudinal studies in this area, Watson, Kumar, and Michaelsen (1993) found that groups that were heterogeneous with respect to culture initially performed, on a series of business case exercises, more poorly than culturally homogeneous groups. As group members gained experience with each other over time, however, performance differences between culturally homogeneous and heterogeneous groups largely disappeared. This is exactly what my colleague Felix Brodbeck has found in studies of multicultural groups in Aston Business School (Brodbeck, Lee, & Overend, 2003; Nisbett, Peng, Choi, & Norenzayan, 2001).

What emerges from much research into cultural diversity is that decision making is improved in groups with members from both collectivist cultures (such as China or Japan) and those from individualist cultures (such as the UK and the Netherlands). The former tend to adopt dialectical approaches to decisions, seeing both sides of every argument. The latter tend to take more extreme decisions on issues, adopting clear "yes" or "no" positions. By combining these two orientations, there is more comprehensive processing of decision issues in multicultural groups representing both collectivist and individualist cultures (Leung, Lu, & Liang, 2003).

Overall, the research on cultural diversity suggests that the norming and storming phases in culturally diverse teams are extended, but that if these teams can learn to work with and integrate their differing perspectives, they are more effective and innovative than homogenous teams. The devil is in the discovery of how to learn to work and integrate their differing perspectives, and this is the subject of most of the rest of this book.

◆ Implications of Diversity

Creating teams involves more than simply assembling the range of skills required for task completion. It also involves thinking through what types of personalities are going to be required to ensure team effectiveness. Moreover, we need to consider the extent to which prospective team members have the basic team working skills (communication, conflict management) that are required for effective team performance. Teams should also have a sufficient level of diversity in members' functional backgrounds, life experience, cultures, and work experience to ensure a variety of perspectives is taken in their work and decision making. This diversity will translate into effectiveness and sparkling innovation, but only if team members can learn to manage their differences as a valuable asset rather than as a threat to their individual identities. Teams of like-minded clones will experience a comfortable existence but will be ineffective and creatively stagnant.

Team leaders should be selected, in part, for their ability to deal with these team composition effects – that is, their ability to enhance the positive effects of heterogeneity and reduce its negative effects. This requires the ability to mobilize team members under a common banner. Strategies may include: the articulation by the leader of clear team-based goals, the use of socialization tactics that focus on what team members have in common rather than how they differ, and the development of mentoring relationships (Anderson & Thomas, 1996). Team leaders will need to be able to do all this while, at the same time, maintaining the differentiation among roles that provide team members with a sense of their unique contribution to the team. Above all, they need to facilitate the exploration and integration of diverse and often conflicting viewpoints in ways that enable teams to derive synergistic benefits from their diversity. It is these strategies and skills we now turn to.

key revision points:

- What are the main stages of team development?

- What personality types are associated with effective team performance?

- Does complementarity of personality types predict team effectiveness?

- What are the main areas of knowledge and skills that are necessary for effective teamwork?

- How does diversity of functional backgrounds affect team effectiveness, innovation, and the relations among team members?

- How do age, gender, and cultural diversity affect team working?

FURTHER READING

Joshi, A. & Jackson, S. E. (2003). Managing workforce diversity to enhance cooperation in organizations. In M. A. West, D. Tjosvold, & K. G. Smith (eds.), *International handbook of organizational teamwork and cooperative working* (pp. 277–96). Chichester, UK: Wiley.

Maznevski, M. L. (1994). Understanding our differences: Performance in decision making groups with diverse members. *Human Relations*, 47: 531–52.

Paulus, P. B. (2000). Groups, teams and creativity: The creative potential of idea-generating groups. *Applied Psychology: An International Review*, 49, 237–62.

Stevens, M. J. & Campion, M. A. (1994). The knowledge, skill, and ability requirements for teamwork: Implications for human resource management. *Journal of Management*, 20, 503–30.

Tjosvold, D. (1998). Cooperative and competitive goal approaches to conflict: Accomplishments and challenges. *Applied Psychology: An International Review*, 47, 285–342.

West, M. A. (2002). Sparkling fountains or stagnant ponds: An integrative model of creativity and innovation implementation in work groups. *Applied Psychology: An International Review*, 51 (3), 355–87.

◆ chapter three

Leading Teams

*Drive, ability, and constitution come together to make leaders
. . . the most successful are able to conjure visions through
their words and infect others with their confidence . . . they
inspire trust by showing they share people's values and
concerns . . . these qualities don't just apply to the good guys:
many of the greatest villains in history were charismatic.*
(Nicholson, 2000, p. 108)

key learning points:

- The three central tasks of the team leader
- The skills of leading teams
- The skills of managing teams
- The skills of coaching team members
- The trip wires that confront team leaders
- How to develop team leadership skills
- Transformational versus transactional leadership

◆ The Three Team Leadership Tasks

The team leader has three overall tasks to perform: to create the
conditions that enable the team to do its job, to build and maintain
the team as a performing unit, and to coach and support the team to
success (see Hackman, 2002 for an extended exploration of these
three tasks).

First, creating the right conditions means ensuring that the team
has a clear task to perform (and one that is best done by a team) and
making sure the team has the resources it needs to do its work. This
means that sometimes the leader has to fight to ensure the team gets

the necessary budget, accommodation, IT equipment, or other tools to do its job effectively. The team leader does not need to be wonderfully bountiful in this since that encourages waste and inefficiency. But the leader should be adamant and unapologetic about arguing for the resources the team needs to get its job done. It is also important for the team's members to be clear about who is and isn't in the team – the boundaries of the team. Some health care teams are composed of core members who work together every day and have others who join the team for perhaps half a day every two weeks (such as medical oncologists in breast cancer care teams). In a warm but misguided attempt to ensure inclusion, leaders often include these visitors as team members and try to involve them in the team as much as possible. It is better to designate people clearly as either core team members or peripheral team members. The team is its core members. The peripheral members work with the team from time to time but cannot operate as full team members because they are simply not together with the others enough. Creating inappropriate expectations about the team's boundaries is a recipe for conflict. Moreover, as we discussed earlier, teams should not exceed six to eight members.

Second, in order to build and maintain the team as a performing unit the leader must ensure that the team is composed of members with the necessary skills and abilities (see chapter 2 on creating teams). And the team must be sufficiently diverse. A team of people who are simply clones of the leader will be neither effective nor innovative. The leader must also develop team processes that help the team to perform effectively by nurturing good decision making, problem solving, and conflict management, and the development of new and improved ways of working together. Good team working doesn't occur naturally. It takes practice. Following one world cup, promoters formed a team from the very best players of all the sides to tour Europe to play exhibition matches. They lost every game they played. Why? Because they were excellent individually but had not learned to work as a team. The leader's job is to encourage the team to practice teamwork so they do learn to work as a team.

The third task of the team leader is to coach and support the team to success. It means intervening to help the team do its work successfully by giving direction and support. The team leader has to learn to be sensitive to the mood of the team and to how well members are interacting and communicating with each other. The leader must pay attention to these processes and intervene to encourage more meetings between particular members, encourage more exchange of information, or shape a supportive approach to suggestions made by team members. The leader's task also includes helping team members develop their skills and abilities. This means taking time to review what it is they want to achieve, what skills each needs to develop, and creating learning opportunities for them (this could be formal training, visits to other organizations, or learning on the job).

Box 3.1: Team leadership differs from traditional leadership

TEAMWORK IN PRACTICE

Traditional leaders tend to be directive rather than facilitative and advice-giving rather than advice-seeking. They seek to determine rather than integrate views and play a directive rather than supportive role. Effective team leaders share responsibility for the team and encourage team members to take responsibility when things are not going well: "Well, what do you think are the problems here and how should we go about solving them?" They are less likely to exercise control over the final choice when decisions need to be made: "OK, so we need to make a choice now. What should it be?" They will tend to manage the team as a whole (like a sports team in its performance) rather than simply managing the individuals. This means focusing on issues like the general mood in the team – is it anxious, stressed, optimistic, or confident? Team leadership differs most clearly from traditional leadership in that the leader focuses on the team as a whole rather than on just the individuals, and shares responsibility with the team for the team's functioning.

So how can the team leader accomplish these three tasks? In order to answer this question, it is helpful to distinguish between three broad elements of the team leader's role: leading, managing, and coaching.

The Three Elements of Leading Teams

Leading is long-term, focused on strategic direction, and requires thought about issues of people management, power, and control;

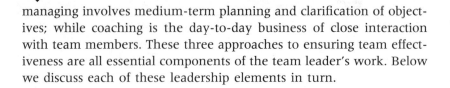

---

managing involves medium-term planning and clarification of objectives; while coaching is the day-to-day business of close interaction with team members. These three approaches to ensuring team effectiveness are all essential components of the team leader's work. Below we discuss each of these leadership elements in turn.

Leading a team

Leading refers to the process of making appropriate strategic interventions in order to motivate and give direction to the team. The team leader encourages team members to work as a team in a collaborative and supportive way, and with a developing sense that the team has the ability and power to accomplish its tasks. Leading involves intuition, fine judgment, and risk. It also demands confidence and even charisma.

Leading involves creating a real team rather than a team in name only. Typically when I ask senior managers about the extent of team working in their organizations, they respond "We're all one big team here" and this may be in organizations of hundreds through to thousands of people! It is heartening when there is a positive and supportive atmosphere in organizations but that is not the same as team working. Leading means quite simply creating the conditions that will produce team success. Leading means creating a compelling direction for the team's work, designing the team in a way that enables it to perform effectively, ensuring the organizational supports are there to enable the team to do its work, and timing leadership interventions carefully. This takes training – in other words leaders have to practice their leadership skills to develop them – a little like developing running skills by training regularly.

Leading involves clearly communicating a compelling direction for the team's work. This is not a democratic process. If it is left to team members to work out, it is likely they will get lost in uncertainty or the confusion of trying to meet multiple aims – the leader's role is to provide overall direction. Consider the elements of the direction this pensions team in a financial advisory organization pursues:

> We aim to provide a service that surprises clients who come to get advice on their pensions. We will achieve that by focusing on what they really need and offering a variety of attractive options in ways that make sense to them. We will do this by working in a team that is supportive, professional and committed to making the work experience of every member positive and stimulating.

The vision their leader paints for the team is challenging and therefore energizes team members' motivation. We respond best to clear and challenging, rather than "do your best," goals (Locke & Latham, 1991). So the vision is also *clear*, since this orients team members and ensures that their work efforts contribute to the team's purpose. Finally, achieving the vision is *consequential* – team members see the value of the vision for clients and for themselves, so they are fully engaged in trying to ensure that the vision becomes reality. As a result, they contribute their knowledge, skill, and creativity to the achievement of the vision.

Leading means designing or sculpting the team in a way that enables it to perform effectively. How can leaders learn to sculpt their teams? They have to practice shaping the task, the authority of the team, the team size, the mix of members, and its tenure. This means designing *the task* to be one that can be performed only by a team working together (such as catching wildebeest on the savannah). The task must be challenging: it will demand a high variety of skills, represent a whole piece of work, and be important for the organization or the wider society. Team leaders give their teams clarity about the *authority* they have to do the work (and the limits of this authority) and give them clear, helpful feedback on team performance. *Team size* will be as small as possible to get the task completed and no more than six to eight members. Team leaders will therefore think about whether the task could be accomplished without loss of quality for customers by having fewer team members. The team will also be *diverse* in terms of members' experience, skills, and functional specialties; diverse in demographic characteristics such as age, gender, and culture; and members will be good team workers – they will have the necessary team-working *knowledge, skills, and attitudes.* They will stay together long enough over the course of their work that they can learn to dance the dance of team work beautifully together – sufficient *tenure* for success. Every six months team leaders should review these dimensions of design and think about whether some redesign of their teams is needed. By practicing these design elements (just like a sculptor or an engineer) leaders will become more and more expert in their team leadership. They will make some mistakes of course, but without mistakes from time to time they cannot develop their skills.

Leading involves winning the organizational supports that enable the team to be successful. This means ensuring appropriate rewards (see chapter 11), the right training for people to work in teams and do their jobs well (see chapter 11), the necessary resources to do the job (e.g., IT equipment, suitable office space), and the information about

Box 3.2: The essence of effective leadership

The essence of effective team leadership is articulating a clear vision and aligning the team around the vision and strategies to achieve it. It means that the leader should communicate enthusiasm, optimism, and excitement about the team's work. The essence of effective leadership is also helping team members to develop their relationships with each other by helping them to appreciate each other, and helping them to learn how to confront and resolve differences constructively and creatively. Growth and development is a powerful human motivation so team leadership requires the leader to help team members to coordinate their activities together, continuously improve their work and performance, and develop their capabilities. Leaders can contribute to this by encouraging them to be flexible in their approach to the team's work (e.g., by experimenting with different ways of working), by objectively analyzing team processes, and collectively learning about better ways to work together. A good team leader will also represent the interests of the team: protecting its reputation; helping to establish trust with other teams, departments, and senior managers; and helping to resolve conflicts creatively between the team and these groups. The leader will also ensure that the team has an identity – celebrating birthdays, celebrating the team's victories, marking departures and arrivals of team members warmly and with rites of passage all contribute to this sense of identity. We fashion our identities from the groups we belong to in and out of work and we need to feel proud of them. The leader plays a key role in this. Much of this requires that leaders have the courage to go against the way things are done in many organizations to offer a better service to clients and to create an environment that is a positive, healthy, and affirming home for team members. Most of all good leadership is about kindness, because that is at the heart of any successful community or team (see West, 2003).

organizational performance and strategy the team needs to be sure it is making the right contribution to the organization. It means ensuring there is all the support the team requires from the organization to enable successful performance and the well-being and growth of team members. Effective team leaders are vigorous in influencing others in the organization to ensure their teams can do their work effectively.

Leading requires timing interventions appropriately to help the team succeed. Teams are most responsive to leader interventions at the beginning of their life, when they have reached a halfway point in their work, when they reach a natural break in their work, or when the "product" has been produced or a performance period has ended (Gersick, 1988, 1989). When a team is getting on with its work and is engaged in the process of doing the job intensively, it is generally a bad time for leader interventions since it disrupts the effectiveness of the group.

Managing a team

The second element of the team leader's role is managing: making sure team members are clear about the objectives of the team, their roles in the team, and their objectives. Managing a team involves ensuring that team objectives, team members' roles, and team structures have been established and are regularly reviewed, and also making certain that formal feedback about team performance is given to team members. Management also involves ensuring team members are clear about how well they are performing.

Managing the team means setting clear shared team objectives. The team has to negotiate its specific objectives linked to the overall compelling direction the leader has set. The manager must ensure that there is a high degree of fit and consistency between organizational objectives, team direction, and team objectives. A statement of those objectives must be laid down in a form that makes the work of the team clear both to itself and to others within the organization, and enables the success of the team to be evaluated.

Managing the team means clarifying the roles of team members. The team leader must manage by ensuring that the role of each team member is clear to all. It is important that each team role is, in part at least, unique to that person, important to the team's work, and contributes to the achievement of team objectives.

Managing the team means developing individual roles. For effective team functioning, individual roles and tasks should be seen by team members as meaningful whole pieces of work, giving them opportunities for growth and development and the exercise of skills (Hackman

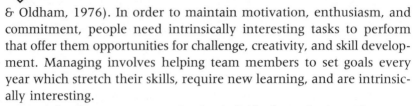
& Oldham, 1976). In order to maintain motivation, enthusiasm, and commitment, people need intrinsically interesting tasks to perform that offer them opportunities for challenge, creativity, and skill development. Managing involves helping team members to set goals every year which stretch their skills, require new learning, and are intrinsically interesting.

Managing the team means evaluating individual contributions. The manager plays a central role in ensuring that individual contributions to overall team objectives are evaluated formally so that people have clear feedback on their performance. Such feedback is usually given on an annual basis, though more frequent feedback is valuable (Murphy & Cleveland, 1995). Individuals also require regular constructive feedback about their performance if they are to grow and develop in their jobs. Traditionally this has taken place via the annual appraisal or review interview in which the individual's superior gives feedback on the year's performance. As flatter structures lead to larger spans of control and each employee's contact network becomes ever wider, this is an increasingly ineffective means of giving team members the feedback they need. Moreover, it is consistent with a team philosophy that the team, and not the team leader, should appraise team members (West & Markiewicz, 2003). The mechanics are straightforward: team members are asked to rate each of the other team members' skills and performance, and feedback is collected (usually via a questionnaire) from the team leader and all team members. The questionnaire assesses performance against predetermined competencies, including team working skills. Answers are then analyzed and feedback is given to the individual.

This approach improves team communication processes, extends ownership and involvement, and enhances the concept of team feedback. This approach to feedback gives the team member an evaluation of their:

- contribution to the output of the team, measured against predetermined targets derived from the team's overall goals;
- performance in their team role;
- contributions in the areas of communication, goal setting, giving feedback to other team members, planning and coordination, collaborative problem solving, conflict resolution, innovation and supportiveness;
- contribution to the team climate or how the team works.

There are a number of ways of providing team member feedback:

- the team leader collects team members' views on predetermined dimensions, collates the information, and gives feedback to the individual;
- at the time of the team performance review, the team also discusses individual performance, sometimes with the help of a facilitator from outside of the team;
- a subgroup of the team is delegated to consider individual aspects of performance and give feedback to individuals on that area only.

The important principles are that the process should help individuals clarify their work objectives; help them to feel valued, respected, and supported; and help them identify the means to achieve any desired personal growth.

Managing the team means providing feedback on team performance. Considerable performance benefits result from the provision of clear and constructive feedback to teams, though this is often an area which team members report is neglected. Team members may get feedback on their performance but team performance is rarely evaluated systematically. In a team-based organization considerable attention should be devoted to the development of performance criteria against which teams can be measured. Teams can be evaluated in relation to:

Team outcomes – the team's performance, be it producing parts, treating patients, or providing customer service – likely to be best defined and evaluated by the "customers" of the teams.

Team viability – the team's sustained ability to work well together. If some team members end up refusing to work with another team member ever again, the team's performance has most probably not been functional. Team members not speaking to another is not a good prognosis for future team performance!

Team member growth and well-being – the learning, development, and satisfaction of team members. In well-functioning teams, members learn from each other constantly.

Team member mental health – the stress or well-being of team members that results directly from their work in the team.

Team innovation – the introduction of new and improved ways of doing things by the team. This is almost the best barometer of team functioning. Teams, by definition, should be fountains of creativity and innovation since they bring together individuals with diverse knowledge, orientations, skills, attitudes, and experiences in a collective enterprise, thus creating the ideal conditions for creativity.

Interteam relations – cooperation with other teams and departments within the organization. Teams must not only be cohesive, they must also cooperate with other teams and departments. Otherwise team cohesion may simply reinforce the steel walls of traditional silos within the organization, undermining collective efforts to achieve organizational goals.

Box 3.3: The fallacies and wisdom of leadership

Smart and brilliant leaders sometimes act foolishly and with disastrous results. Robert Sternberg (2002) has identified four faulty beliefs that can lead to foolishness in leaders, sometimes with disastrous consequences:

The egocentrism fallacy: They believe it's all about them and so only take into account their own interests and needs when making important decisions.

The omniscience fallacy: Leaders may well know a lot about some things but it is a mistake for them to assume they know a lot about everything.

The omnipotence fallacy: They think that they are all powerful and can do what they want, regardless of the legitimacy or morality of their actions.

The invulnerability fallacy: Leaders sometimes think they can get away with whatever they want to do, that they will not be caught out, and even if they are they will be able to get themselves out of it.

Leaders are particularly prone to falling victim to these fallacies because the higher up they go, the more people are respectful, unquestioning and seeking their approval. Wisdom does not necessarily go with the territory. Wisdom is defined as "the use of intelligence and creativity towards a common good through balancing one's own interests, other people's interests and infusing moral and ethical values" (Sternberg, 2003, p. 5).

TEAMWORK IN PRACTICE

Managing means the team leader offering his or her subjective observations about the performance of the team, but most feedback should be based on objective, quantitative, and qualitative data wherever possible. It may also involve seeking feedback from those affected by the team's work. For example, in a primary health care team, the manager might seek feedback in one of various forms: patient satisfaction surveys with the practice, patient satisfaction surveys with clinical interviews, feedback from relatives and carers on the supportiveness of the practice, and feedback from local hospitals on the efficiency of the practice.

Managing means reviewing group processes, strategies, and objectives. A major contributor to effective team performance is "task reflexivity." Task reflexivity is the extent to which a team openly and actively reflects upon and appropriately modifies its objectives, strategies, and processes in order to maximize effectiveness. In other words, teams should regularly take time out to review the methods, objectives, and procedures they are using and modify them as appropriate. Chris Argyris, an American organizational psychologist, has coined the term "double loop learning" to describe the difference between how teams and organizations assess whether they are doing things right, versus whether they are doing the right things. Argyris (1993) argues that many organizations only consider how efficient they are, that is, whether they are doing things right. For example, a manufacturer of metal springs might be spending time focusing on whether the correct amount of tension exists within the springs that are being produced in order to achieve a bigger market rather than developing a completely new type of spring for the changing market. This is focusing on doing things right. Double loop learning involves going a step beyond and asking whether the organization or team is doing the right thing. For example, it may be that the production of computer chips is not the right thing to be doing in a highly competitive market and that the manufacturer should change over to the production of wireless networking systems.

Managing means ensuring that there is a high degree of double loop learning or reflexivity within a team by setting up regular reviews of team objectives, methods, structures, and processes. As a minimum, in complex decision-making teams, reviews should take place at least every six months where the group discusses successes over the previous period, the difficulties encountered, as well as the failures of the team.

It is usually the responsibility of the team manager to set up "time out" from the team's daily work to enable these review processes to take place. While some doubt the wisdom of taking time out from a team's busy work to conduct such reviews, there is strong evidence that teams that do this are far more effective than those that do not (Hackman & Morris, 1975; West, 2000). Often in our work with the management teams of hospitals in the UK, we have found that teams under most pressure are those that are working least effectively and that are consequently least prepared to take time out to review their strategies and processes. It is as though they are running so fast on a treadmill, they are not aware of the opportunities that stepping off affords them, either to go in a different direction or to travel not on a treadmill but on an escalator!

Box 3.4: Favoritism

TEAMWORK IN PRACTICE

Team leaders typically behave in a way that communicates there is an in-group and an out-group within the team. In-group members are those the leader perceives as more competent and likable. Out-group members are those the leader has most difficulty getting on with and who the leader thinks are less competent. The team leader will tend to explain the successes of in-group members in terms of their ability, and their failures to circumstances beyond their control; with out-group members they do exactly the opposite. On reflection leaders recognize that they spend markedly less time talking and meeting with out-group members. What they probably don't realize is that all team members would be able to tell who is "in" and who is "out." This builds resentments and undermines team effectiveness. Leaders must practice spending more time with those team members whose competence they are least confident about or who they find less agreeable to be with. They should coach them and develop their relationships with them by using coaching skills and so build one all-encompassing in-group in the team (Graen & Scandura, 1987).

Coaching a team

Coaching is the facilitation and management of day-to-day team processes, and involves listening rather than administering. Whereas managing focuses on monitoring, giving feedback, and communicating information about the wider organization, coaching is a less formal process in which the coach listens, supports, and offers advice, guidance, and suggestions to team members. Coaching is the day-to-day work the leader undertakes to help the team achieve its objectives and its potential by giving frequent and specific support, encouragement, guidance, and feedback. It is the process of facilitating the individual and collective efforts of members of a team. Think of the football coach on the side of the pitch during the game and that is similar to what the team leader does when coaching. The concept of coaching is based on the idea that there should be both guidance in appropriate directions, and the creation of conditions within which team members can discover for themselves ways of improving work performance. Coaching requires the basic skills of listening, recognizing and revealing feelings, giving feedback, and agreeing goals. We will explore each in detail below.

Listening

This is the principal skill of team coaching and has four elements: active listening, open listening, drawing out, and reflection.

1 *Active listening*. This means putting effort into the listening process. All too often I am aware, when meeting with team members, how easy it is for me to be nodding, looking interested and concerned, but actually to be far away thinking about a previous meeting or, say, a conversation about Harry Potter with my daughter. Active listening means giving active attention to the team member you are with here and now, as well as interpreting what they are saying, that is, listening between the words. It takes practice and practice and practice.

2 *Open listening*. This is listening with an open mind: suspending judgment to let the individual work through an idea. The team leader should not assume he or she knows the answer before the person has presented their problem or told their story. Listening with an open mind involves suspending judgment until the person has had an opportunity to explore the issue thoroughly or to explain the problem issue fully. The best strategy for problem solving is to spend most of the time clarifying the problem before trying to generate solutions. It is clearly not a productive course of action to generate solutions to the wrong problems! *The team leader should therefore encourage team members to explore problems fully rather than offering solutions.* This is very important and hard to practice in reality. For example, in working with hundreds of team managers across Europe who have role-played team coaching, I have found the major challenge they experience is with the temptation to solve problems too quickly. Coaching involves waiting

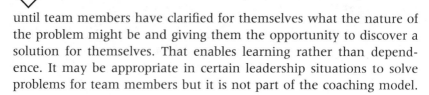
until team members have clarified for themselves what the nature of the problem might be and giving them the opportunity to discover a solution for themselves. That enables learning rather than dependence. It may be appropriate in certain leadership situations to solve problems for team members but it is not part of the coaching model.

3   *Drawing out.* A major part of listening involves encouraging team members to talk about their ideas, feelings, and aspirations. This is helped considerably by asking "open" questions, such as: Why?, How? Who? The purpose is to enable team members to elaborate and articulate their own exploration of a particular problem or issue that they are consulting the team leader about. Closed questions are characterized by whether "yes" and "no" answers can be given in response to them, such as: "Is spending too much time at work causing you problems at home?" An appropriate open question in that situation might be: "How is your current workload causing problems for you?" Again, most aspiring team coaches too readily identify the nature of the problem in their questioning. When a team member tells the leader that he or she is spending too much time at work, the leader may make the mistake of asking what appears to be an open question, but is in fact a closed and leading question such as: "Why are you having difficulties prioritizing your work?" What a more effective team coach could ask is: "Why do you think this is happening?" "What sorts of pressures do you feel you are currently under?" "How do you feel about it?"

4   *Reflective listening.* This involves restating your understanding of what a team member has said to you. Essentially it involves summarizing their previous statements, for example: "So you're saying despite enjoying your work, you feel you want to have more freedom to define and pursue new projects on your own?" Again, this interpretation should not be the team leader's definition of the nature of the problem, it should be a genuine attempt to restate and summarize the information given by the team member. This is a very powerful form of coaching that enables team members to explore particular issues in their team work more thoroughly. Reflective listening is powerful for the following reasons:

- It ensures that you listen actively to what the team member is saying.
- It communicates to the team member your genuine desire to understand what he or she is saying.
- It gives you the opportunity to correct your misunderstandings.

- It enables you to be confident that you have correctly understood what the team member is saying.
- It builds mutual empathy and understanding.

You may be concerned that simply restating information offered by team members will appear to be an empty, parrot-like process. Research on interaction processes has demonstrated that such summarizing statements normally encourage others to elaborate further on the information already given, rather than simply affirming the correctness of what was said. Exploration is facilitated rather than curtailed by reflective listening.

Recognizing and revealing feelings

If a team leader is to facilitate team members' work and experiences, the whole person must be encompassed and not just those parts of them that are perceived as comfortable to deal with. It is sometimes appropriate and necessary to spend time exploring and clarifying the feelings of team members if team leaders are to perform their tasks effectively. This also demands revealing their feelings and being comfortable and clear about doing that. Team leaders will be the object of frustration or anger from time to time and will themselves occasionally feel frustrated and angry with team members. Dealing with those feelings in an appropriate way, and at the right times, is an important part of coaching.

What I am not suggesting is that team leaders should explore every nuance of team members' emotional reactions and frustrations. Where there are major "feelings" issues team members should be given an opportunity to express and explore those feelings. Team members who are feeling overloaded and frustrated with their colleagues may need some space to express that frustration before they are able to analyze the balance of tasks and priorities currently facing them. It is often the case that by focusing on feelings, the facts emerge, whereas when the focus is on facts, the feelings often remain hidden and unexpressed. The expression of such emotions has a useful impact not just on people's immediate well-being but also on their ability to deal with similar stresses in the future.

Leaders should express their emotions in a constructive nonblaming way:

> I'm feeling frustrated because after our last team meeting I promised the customer we would deliver the order by tonight, and it's looking as if we may not be able to do that. I feel embarrassed about letting them

vn and frustrated because we agreed we were able to achieve this with ease. Can we discuss as a team what has gone wrong and what we can learn from this?

Such expressions are much more likely to be accepted if 95 percent or more of a team leader's emotional expressions are warm, positive, and encouraging. The task of a team leader is to create a positive and enthusiastic emotional climate, since this will enable the team to be creative and cooperative in its work.

Giving feedback

Feedback is a word that is widely used in organizations but often misunderstood and rarely practiced. Feedback involves giving clear reactions to specific behaviors in a sensitive and constructive way. When Nigel Nicholson and I conducted a survey of over 2,000 British managers we found that most criticized their organizations for not giving them positive feedback about their work (Nicholson & West, 1988). When we then asked managers to analyze their own time use we found that they prioritized giving positive feedback to their own team members almost at the bottom of their list of activities!

Giving feedback means being specific and focusing on team members' behavior and the consequences of their behavior. For example:

> I noticed that you stopped the group from reaching agreement about the inclusion of that set of questions in the marketing survey because you had a sense that they were not appropriate. This was in the face of some frustration from other team members. However, the consequence was that a much better set of questions was achieved and will provide us with more useful information as a result.

In this instance, feedback focuses on a particular example of behavior and the positive consequences of it. Feedback is not about patting people on the head and giving them "smiley faces." That can be patronizing and implies the team coach has a parental type of power over the individual. Rather, feedback should be aimed at consolidating and improving performance within the team.

Feedback is most effective in changing and strengthening behavior when it follows immediately after the behavior. Within organizations feedback is often withheld until the annual appraisal meeting. This has very limited impact on behavior. The team leader (and indeed all team members) should provide feedback for team members on a daily basis.

Positive feedback is much more effective in changing behavior than negative feedback. It is better to ensure a very strong balance of positive against negative feedback (95% to 5% is getting to the right sort of balance). But because we are quicker to recognize the discrepancies between actual and desired behavior in the workplace, the balance is often inappropriately in favor of negative feedback. This is a consequence of our normal reaction to our environment. We tend to see discrepancy when what we expect and what actually occurs do not match. Consequently the team leader has to be alert and attentive to spot the constant examples of consistency – when there is a match between expectations and reality – rather than discrepancy, and then to provide feedback as a result.

Agreeing goals

The number one task of a team leader is to constantly ensure the team and its members are clear about the team's direction, its objectives, and individual team members' goals. It is a fundamental principle of work behavior that goal setting has a powerful influence on performance (Locke & Latham, 1991). The role of the team leader must involve helping team members clarify and agree goals. If, for example, a team member is concerned about workload, part of coaching should be to facilitate a shared agreement about goals between the team leader, the other team member, and the concerned individual. Making sure there is a fair balance of workloads among team members is very important for team effectiveness. Equally, ensuring that no-one is so overloaded that they are unable to cope is the team leader's (and all team members') responsibility.

◆ Trip Wires for Team Leaders

Richard Hackman (1990, 2002) has identified five hidden trip wires that can cause team leaders to fail:

1 *Call the performing unit a team, but really manage members as individuals* Individual responsibilities within a team can be assigned and then individual activities are coordinated by the team leader so that the sum of team members' efforts combines to form the whole team product. The second strategy is to assign a team task and give team members responsibility for determining how that task should be completed. Hackman argues that a mixed model, where people are told they are a team but are treated as individuals, with individual performance appraisal and individual rewards, confuses team members

and leads to team ineffectiveness. Individual performance is rewarded with bonuses but team performance is given no attention. Similarly, the careers of individual team members are managed separately and sometimes even in competition with one another. Consequently team working is inhibited since team members are likely to compete to achieve their individual goals rather than to cooperate with one another toward achieving shared goals.

> To reap the benefits of team work, one must actually build a team. Calling a set of people a team or exhorting them to work together is insufficient. Instead, explicit action must be taken to establish the team's boundaries, to define the task as one for which members are collectively responsible and accountable, and to give members the authority to manage both their internal processes and the team's relations with external entities such as clients and co-workers.
>
> **(Hackman, 1990, p. 495)**

2 *"Fall off the authority balance beam"*
Exercising authority in teams creates anxiety for team members and for team leaders. Inappropriate ways of resolving that anxiety are sometimes to exercise excessive leadership and sometimes to exercise too little. Leadership involves exercising authority in some areas and withholding it in others; or conversely, giving autonomy in some areas but withholding it in others. Team leaders should be unapologetic about exercising authority to ensure that direction is achieved for the team's work, since this is such a fundamental contributor to team effectiveness. At the same time teams should be given the authority, within obvious boundaries, to determine the means by which they achieve their ends. Ensuring that the team has set itself a clear direction empowers rather than disempowers the team. One can "fall off the authority balance beam" by giving a team too much autonomy or leeway by not providing sufficient direction; the result is that the team wallows in uncertainty and lacks motivation and commitment. Alternatively, the team leader can exercise too much authority and prevent the team from operating as a team altogether. A typical mistake is giving a team too much authority early in its life when direction is needed, and then intervening too heavily later when the team is not performing well.

3 *Simply assemble a large group*
Where group composition is unclear or vague and where structures and responsibilities have not been worked out, team members may fall victim to the kinds of process losses such as the social loafing and

free-rider effects that were described earlier. Hackman argues that three important elements are necessary to ensure a suitable structure for a team. First is a *well-designed team task* that represents a meaningful and motivating piece of work accompanied by a sufficient degree of autonomy for team members to be able to conduct the work successfully and get direct feedback about the results of their efforts. Second is a *well-assembled team* that should be as small as possible while enabling the team to get the job done efficiently, and that has the appropriate mix of skills and resources within the team. Third, the team should have *very clear, explicit, and unambiguous information* about the extent and limits of its authority and accountability so that team members do not stray into areas beyond their scope or make decisions that are not appropriate for them to make.

4 *Specify challenging team objectives but skimp on organizational support*
Teams in organizations are sometimes given "stretch" objectives that require them to achieve ever more challenging targets. This can be very useful in improving performance and giving team members a sense of challenge. But if organizations give inadequate organizational resources then teams will be unlikely to get their work done. The key resources are:

- a reward system that recognizes and rewards excellent team performance, not just individual performance;
- an educational system within the organization that provides the necessary training in skills to enable the team to achieve its objectives;
- an information system that provides the team with the kinds of data that will enable them to achieve their objectives and in an adequate form;
- the material resources that will enable them to get the work done, such as money, computing equipment, congenial space, and staff.

These systems and resources are described in more detail in chapter 11 (see also West & Markiewicz, 2003).

It is my own observation that in many organizations there is little thought given to how teams rather than individuals can be rewarded or how teams can be provided with the resources and information that they need. This is despite the fact that team-based organizations are becoming much more the norm within both the public and private sectors. There is also very little training given to people for working in and managing teams despite the fact that teamwork is now considered such a basic building block of functioning organizations.

Leaders must therefore work hard to exercise upward and lateral influence to ensure that appropriate support systems are available for teams within organizations.

5 *Assume that members already have all the competence they need to work well as a team*
Team leaders have to make process interventions to improve the effectiveness of teams from time to time. The point at which they intervene is very important also. Team leaders must take the time to coach and help team members and the team as a whole through periods of difficulty as well as through periods of success, and it is a mistake to assume that team members are competent to deal with new challenges as they come up. Team leadership involves constant awareness of the processes in teams and active intervention to improve them at appropriate times. Team work is not blind democracy but a constant learning about how to dance more creatively and effectively together.

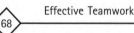 **Developing Team Leadership Skills**

At least once a year team leaders should ask their team members to give them feedback on how well they are accomplishing their leadership tasks:

- "To what extent have I provided a clear direction for your work?"
- "Are you excited and motivated by the work we do?"
- "Does the team task really require a team to do it?"
- "To what extent does the task stretch us and require us to use our skills to full effect? How could the work we do be made more challenging and motivating?"
- "To what extent do I give enough authority to you for you to get on and be successful as a team?"
- "To what extent do I give you sufficient information about how well the team is performing?"
- "Do I time my interventions to help the team work well appropriately or do I come across as interfering [always ask for examples]?"
- "Do we have enough team members to do the job effectively?"
- "To what extent do we have the resources, information, accommodation, and training to accomplish our task?"
- "To what extent are you satisfied with the rewards you get as a team for the work you do (rather than individual rewards)?"

Box 3.5: Emotional intelligence: Developing self-awareness

Your emotional intelligence determines your success as a leader (Goleman, 2002). This has four elements: self-awareness, self-management (learning to control your impulses), social awareness (empathy), and managing relationships. How can you develop self-awareness, the first and most important element of emotional intelligence?

1 Start to keep a diary of how you felt during the course of each working day, noting your overall mood, how you felt when talking with specific team members, or during team meetings. Note when you felt emotionally positive and negative and why.

2 Read through the diary at the end of each week and look for any patterns in the flow of your feelings so that you can become more aware of the patterns of your emotions.

3 Practice mindfulness each day also. Try to catch yourself 10 times a day and note how you are feeling. In other words, just like an athlete, train your self-awareness.

4 Take time out once each day for 20 to 30 minutes quiet reflection. You can do this by closing your office door to others and blocking phone calls. Or you can take a walk alone to give you the peace and stillness to reflect.

5 Consider learning meditation and practicing once or twice a day. First thing in the morning and before your evening meal are good times (or even on train journeys or flights). Meditation automatically develops your self-awareness.

6 As you arrive at work each day, note how you feel: are you optimistic, confident, enthusiastic or down, anxious or angry?

7 Remember that your job as a manager and leader is to help those you lead by not indulging your moods. So practice being positive in your approach to life and work, by being enthusiastic and optimistic, and – most important – encourage good humor and laughter.

8 Think positive and you will feel positive.

TEAMWORK IN PRACTICE

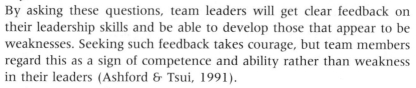
By asking these questions, team leaders will get clear feedback on their leadership skills and be able to develop those that appear to be weaknesses. Seeking such feedback takes courage, but team members regard this as a sign of competence and ability rather than weakness in their leaders (Ashford & Tsui, 1991).

There are two dominant styles of leadership called transformational and transactional (Howell & Avolio, 1993; Yukl, 1998). Leaders can develop their leadership by nurturing a transformational style of leadership. Transactional leaders focus on transactions – exchanges and rewards or punishments for team members in order to change their behavior. Their focus is primarily on the task and ensuring a high level of performance among those they lead. Transformational leaders encourage team members by influencing them to transform their views of themselves and their work. Transformational leaders rely on charisma and the ability to conjure inspiring visions of the future. They use emotional or ideological appeals to change the behavior of the team, moving them from self-interest in work values to thinking of the whole team and how they can help the organization. Both styles are effective since inspiration or reward can lead to effective team performance, but being able to shift between styles as the situation requires helps leaders manage their teams most effectively. Most leaders, however, rely on a transactional style, which is likely to be less effective when used alone. Transformational leadership appears generally more effective as a team leadership style (Bass, 1990; Howell & Avolio, 1993).

You can develop your transformational leadership by nurturing charisma. That means learning to be optimistic (not unrealistic), and expressing positive emotions in the form of enthusiasm, excitement, appreciation, pleasure, contentment, and celebration rather than negative emotions such as anger, anxiety, discontent, and irritation. Bring positive energy to work and those around you will be affected by your energy. Moodiness is particularly damaging to becoming more transformational. Transformational leadership also involves stimulating team members by painting for them an attractive and compelling picture of what they can accomplish and the means to accomplish it. This means consistently thinking through what it is the team is trying to achieve; developing wise and effective plans for success; and then communicating, discussing, and selling these plans to your team. They will have an increased awareness of their tasks and the importance of them to the organization, and will be motivated to achieve the goals and to performing their tasks well. Moreover they will be motivated to work for the good of the team and the organization and not just their own personal gain or benefit.

You will transform your team members too by devoting a good part of your considerable energy to thinking through how to help them develop their knowledge, skills, abilities, and careers, and discussing and planning this with them. By doing this you focus them on their own development, increase their skills and confidence, and satisfy one of the basic human needs – the need to grow, develop, and discover through engaging with our environments. And of course, that means they are likely to perform to a much higher level and to be more satisfied in their work as a consequence (West, 2003).

Box 3.6: Fitting leadership style to the situation

TEAMWORK IN PRACTICE

Another way of thinking of team leadership is in terms of four overall styles: directive, achievement-oriented, supportive, and facilitative. The first two are primarily transactional and the last two more transformational. Choosing one depends partly on your own personality but it should also be appropriate for the situation. This is a combination of the task the team has to perform (how clear and predictable it is) and the strength of the team members in skills, motivation, and confidence.

Choose a directive transactional style, set goals, and give guidance and rewards as appropriate when the task your team members must perform is not clear or straightforward and they do not have a high level of skill or confidence in the task.

Select an achievement-orientated (transactional) style by setting challenging goals and communicating your expectations that your team members will perform at the highest level. Reward for achievement. Use this style when the task is very clear, and your team members have a high level of skill, ability, and motivation for the task.

A supportive (transformational) style that involves showing concern for followers is more appropriate when the task is very clear and predictable but the team members have a low level of skill, ability, confidence, or motivation.

Finally a participative (transformational) style, which is characterized by the leader consulting with team members before making decisions, is most appropriate when the task is unclear and complex, but the team members have a high level of skill relevant to the task and are highly motivated.

A word of warning about charisma and self-esteem: charismatic leaders who are motivated primarily by their own needs for self-advancement and simply use team members to help achieve their own ends are precisely those who most spectacularly derail in organizations (and in history). They are the equivalent of religious cult leaders who are more concerned with using followers to confirm their self-image and beliefs, rather than to help their followers. Check that your decisions are designed to meet the needs of your clients and your team members first and foremost.

What all leaders must develop, if they do not already possess this quality, is humility. Personally this means we have to be aware of our own inadequacies and the strengths of others and that our power should not lead us to assume that we can behave in inconsiderate, arrogant, or insensitive ways. An old Zen prescription for all, and it applies particularly to leaders, is "keep don't know mind; only keep don't know mind."

◆ Self-managing or Self-leading Work Teams

Much of the discussion in this chapter has implied that leadership, management, or coaching is the remit of one member of the team. It is certainly more convenient to describe management and leadership in this way, but it is important for the leader to be aware that every member of the team should take responsibility for managing, coaching, and leading. If team members evade their own responsibilities for direction, support, influencing, and authority in the team, it is likely that the team will be less effective. On the football pitch, all team members encourage, support, advise, guide, and berate each other throughout the game to ensure the team's success. They do not simply rely on the captain or the coach. Managing meetings, for example, is the responsibility of each person in the team. When a team member sees the team going in what they think is an inappropriate direction, it is his or her responsibility to speak up if team effectiveness is to be maximized.

This chapter has examined team leadership and it is clear there is no simple prescription for managing or leading teams. Being democratic or authoritarian, supportive or directive, hands-off or hands-on, are all necessary elements of the role of those leading the team. Much depends on the time in a team's life, the stage of the projects it is pursuing, the organizational context within which it is working, the individual personalities and skills of team members, and the personality of those delegated to be team leaders.

Team leadership is the responsibility of all team members and that responsibility should not be abrogated in situations where one person is designated as team leader. The promise of effective managing, coaching, and leadership is that the skills and abilities of diverse individuals can be molded together to produce excellent team performance, in which the ideal of synergy is created in practice. As those who have worked in successful teams will know, the consequences in personal satisfaction, the sense of competence and collegiality are enhanced considerably, and the sense of being part of an effective dynamic unit is indeed a rewarding one.

key revision points

- What are the three main tasks of the team leader and why are they so important?

- How does traditional leadership differ from team leadership?

- What does leading a team involve and how does this differ from managing and coaching a team? How does it affect the performance of the team?

- What are the main tasks involved in managing a team and why are they important for team effectiveness?

- What are the main skills involved in coaching a team and why are they important for team effectiveness?

- What are the main trip wires confronting team leaders and how can they be avoided?

- What is the difference between transformational and transactional approaches to leading teams?

- In what situations are directive, achievement-oriented, supportive, and participative styles of team leadership most effective and why?

FURTHER READING

Bass, B. (1990). *Bass & Stogdill's handbook of leadership: Theory, research and managerial applications* (3rd edn.). New York: Free Press.

Hackman, J. R. (2002). *Leading teams: Setting the stage for great performances.* Cambridge, MA: Harvard Business School Press.

House, R. J. & Mitchell, T. R. (1974). A path goal theory of leadership. *Journal of Contemporary Business, 5,* 81–94.

Kanter, R. M. (1983). *The change masters.* New York: Simon and Schuster.

Nicholson, N. (2000). *Managing the human animal.* London: Texere.

West, M. A. (2003). *The secrets of successful teams.* London: Duncan Baird.

Yukl, G. (1998). *Leadership in organizations* (4th edn.). London: Prentice Hall.

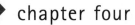

chapter four

Team Building

Start the day with a Raft Building & Racing Teambuilding event designed to get you thinking, communicating and working together. The competitive theme continues with the afternoon paintballing activities. Here resource management is introduced with a limit of 500 included paintball rounds per individual. Teamwork, leadership & good communication skills are required to win the day. Points are accumulated throughout the day.

Combat Games Ltd, 2002.
www.paintball-games.co.uk

We trained hard, but it seemed every time we were beginning to form up into teams, we would be reorganized. I was to learn later in life that we tend to meet any new situation by reorganizing, and a wonderful method it can be for creating the illusion of progress while producing confusion, inefficiency and demoralization.

(From Petronius Arbiter, *Satyricon*, AD 66)

---

key learning points:

■ The effect of team building on team effectiveness and team member attitudes

■ The five main types of team building

■ How to run team-building sessions

■ Topics to be covered in away days

■ Role clarification and negotiation

Parallel to the development of the team as a principal functional unit of organizations has come the development of a myriad of team-building interventions offered by consultants, popular books, and personnel specialists. However, reviews of the effectiveness of team-building interventions have shown that, while they often have a reliable effect upon team members' attitudes to one another, there is little impact upon team task performance (Tannenbaum, Salas, & Cannon-Bowers, 1996). How do we reconcile the contradiction between the increase in the number of team-building interventions offered and the lack of evidence justifying their effectiveness?

Most team-building interventions focus on team relationships and cohesiveness, and are based on the mistaken assumption that improvements in cohesiveness lead to improvements in team task performance. In the few interventions that have focused primarily on task issues there does appear to be some improvement in task-related performance, though not consistently so. In this chapter, therefore, a clear distinction is drawn between team task processes and team social processes.

Teams exist to do a job, to perform a task. Some 200,000 years ago it was catching wildebeest on the savannah. Today it may be providing postal services for a rural area or health care for an inner-city community. Whether team members like each other is much less relevant to their catching the wildebeest than whether they are clear about each other's roles. They need to understand which team members will drive the herd across the plain, which will identify the beast to target, and which team members will hide behind the rocks ready to leap out and spear the target beast. Moreover, they have to share an understanding of the implicit strategy here. Whether they feel warm and friendly toward one another is largely irrelevant to their success in catching the wildebeest and so having enough food for the community to survive.

Teams that are successful become more cohesive – our liking increases for those with whom we experience success (Mullen & Copper, 1994). Cohesive teams are not necessarily successful. Cohesive teams may collude not to work hard in an organization; or they may be more concerned with everyone agreeing and being warm to one another than with vigorously debating how to give the best service to customers. Success breeds cohesion. Failure lowers morale (Worchel, Lind, & Kaufman, 1975).

We need to clarify the type of team-building intervention required when working with teams and then identify very specific objectives, rather than assuming that a general intervention will have generally beneficial effects. Many team-building interventions are based on the expectation that a day or two of team building will lead to dramatic improvements in team functioning. It is equivalent to hoping that one session of psychotherapy will change a person's life dramatically.

The evidence suggests that it is continual interaction and effort that lead to improvements in functioning, rather than any "quick fix."

◆ Types of Team-building Interventions

Team-building interventions can be divided into five main types, each requiring a very different approach. Before beginning an intervention a team should therefore satisfy itself about the type of team-building intervention required.

Team start-up

This type of team building is specific to a team that is just beginning its work and that requires clarification of its objectives, strategies, processes, and roles. The beginning of a team's life has a significant influence on its later development and effectiveness, especially when crises occur. Start-up interventions can help create team ethos, determine clarity of direction, and shape team working practices. Many of the issues that should be dealt with in a start-up intervention were covered in chapters 1 and 2. They include:

- ensuring the team has a whole and meaningful task to perform;
- clarifying team objectives;
- ensuring that each team member has a whole, meaningful, and intrinsically interesting task to perform;
- ensuring that team members' activities can be evaluated;
- ensuring that team performance as a whole is monitored and that team members are given regular and clear feedback on individual *and* team performance;
- establishing a means for regular communication and review within the team (Guzzo, 1996).

It is ambitious to introduce established procedures in all areas of a team's functioning at its inception. Rather, effort should go in to: determining the overall task and objectives for the team; clarifying objectives and interrelated roles for team members; building in performance feedback for individual team members and the team as a whole; and establishing mechanisms for regular communication and review of all aspects of team functioning.

Regular formal reviews

Formal reviews usually take the form of "away days" of one or two days' duration during which the team reviews objectives, roles, strategies, and processes in order to maintain and promote effective functioning.

As in any other area of human activity, regular review of functioning can lead to greater awareness of strengths, skills, weaknesses, and problem areas, and future functioning being improved. Whether for individuals, couples, families, teams, or organizations, there is value in stepping back from ongoing day-to-day processes, examining areas of activity, and reflecting upon the appropriateness of existing ways of doing things. Within work teams, regular away days are a useful way of ensuring a team's continuing effectiveness. Indeed there is much evidence that teams that take time out to review processes are more effective than those that do not.

When should a team take time out for an away day? When a team is involved in completing its work effectively and busy with task-related issues, an away day to review activities can be disruptive. A good time to schedule an away day is when a team has completed a major component of its work. However, if away days are regularly established, for example, on a six-monthly basis, then these need not interfere with the team's normal functioning since they are expected and can be used to deal with specific issues identified by the team. Away days should be of at least one full day's duration since there is usually more to talk about than is anticipated. Two days is ideal for most teams, but in some cases, this may be perceived as a luxury.

There is great advantage in conducting away days in comfortable locations away from the team's normal working environment. I have conducted team-building sessions for BP Oil Europe in the luxurious Brussels Sodehotel in Belgium. The drawback was that the hotel was located a mere 220 yards from BP Oil Europe's headquarters, and team members would sometimes "slip out" to attend to an "urgent" matter of business. It is therefore wise to hold team sessions well away from the demands of the place of work to avoid such interruptions. At the same time, there is much to be said for the kind of comfort and facilities provided in hotels and conference venues. Having a good supply of flip charts, pens, paper, and post-it notes, as well as good food and pleasant surroundings, can make the team work enjoyable and pleasurable, especially for those who are reluctant to attend initially. Both the financial commitment and the time invested in a well-conducted focused away day is more than amply remunerated by the returns in performance that accrue.

All team members should attend away days and, where possible, a facilitator should be commissioned. Facilitators enable team leaders and other team members to focus on the content of the day, without being distracted by responsibility for the processes. Also, a facilitator can sometimes provide an outside view of processes and comment on apparent diversions or blockages. Facilitators should be chosen with care. They should have experience of team interventions and be knowledgeable about team processes. Ideally the facilitator will be a psychologist who can provide evidence of team development work in other organizational settings, and who would be prepared to give the names of contacts in organizations who could vouch for the effectiveness of their intervention work. The facilitator should have a good knowledge of the relevant research literature on teams at work. He or she should also be able to advise on how to evaluate the effectiveness of the interventions. For qualified facilitators in the UK who are highly skilled in developing effective teams contact info@astonod.com.

Away days must be carefully planned, but with a sufficient degree of flexibility to allow emerging topics to be dealt with appropriately. Having a well-structured program of activities is essential for a productive away day. It is useful to have a mix of individual work, pairs work, syndicate work, and whole group work. Individual work is often necessary to enable team members to clarify their thoughts and reactions to various issues before being exposed to the melting pot of the whole group. Pairs work is an invaluable way of ensuring that all team members are encouraged to be active in the process of reviewing activities. It is also much less threatening for some team members than working in larger groups. Syndicate work involves small sub-groups of the team working together, and this can encourage team members who do not normally work together to share their knowledge and expertise. Finally, whole group work is valuable in ensuring that the whole team has ownership of outcomes. It also minimizes suspicions about any secret deals and political maneuverings that might be taking place.

What topics or what content should be dealt with? There is little value in trying to cover every topic in one day. Changing behavior is extremely difficult, and trying to change complex teams in one session is nearly impossible. Away days should focus on a limited range of topics, such as objectives and communication. One indication that an away day intervention has attempted to cover too many areas is when the end of the day is rushed and action plans are ill-specified and badly formulated.

Topics to be covered in an away day can include:

- team successes and difficulties in the previous six-month or one-year period and what can be learned from them;
- a review of team objectives and their appropriateness;
- the roles of team members;
- quality of team communication;
- team interaction frequency;
- team meetings, how valuable they are, and what needs to be changed to improve them;
- team decision-making processes;
- excellence in the team's work;
- support for innovation;
- team social support;
- conflict resolution in the team;
- support for personal growth and development.

Addressing known task-related problems

In order to deal with specific known problem issues the team must take time out to define carefully the task-related problem it is confronting. Then the team develops alternative options for overcoming the problem, and action plans for implementing the selected way forward.

Where a specific problem can be identified and team members are satisfied they have correctly identified the nature of the problem and not simply a symptom of a deeper unresolved team issue, it is useful to take time out for focused intervention. The content and process of the intervention depends very much on the nature of the problem. If it is one to do with objectives, participation, commitment to excellence, or support for innovation, then the exercises described in Chapters 6 to 8 of this book can be used. If it concerns the social elements of team functioning, the material described in Chapter 9 should be employed. In some circumstances, however, the nature of the problem will require a facilitator to help the team.

In the example in Box 4.1, a known problem was handled by a team in ways which led to improvement in team relationships and functioning. It was an indication of the success of the day that the whole team, including Wendy, decided subsequently to set up regular away days for the team in the future.

Box 4.1: Dealing with a known problem

Wendy was the assistant team leader in a voluntary organization's personnel department. She wanted a team-building workshop because of problems of team divisiveness and hostility. After background briefing to a facilitator on the history of the team, its tenure, and its composition, the facilitator gave questionnaires to team members that included questions asking them to indicate what they saw as the major barriers to team functioning. Examination of the responses revealed a strong sense of dissatisfaction with Wendy as a leader. Most team members described her as being overly directive, bureaucratic, and inclined to have favorites. A number of team members also felt that she was guilty of talking behind their backs about their "poor performance." This, they claimed, had led to bad feeling on the part of both Wendy's favorites and those seen as her victims. Wendy was in her first management position and felt uncertain and anxious, which may have contributed to her directive style and tendency to reward and punish inappropriately.

A day was set aside for a team-building intervention to examine the team processes. Wendy failed to turn up, phoning in to say she was ill. Nevertheless, the team decided to address the issue and discussed how they should function on that day, given the complication of Wendy's nonattendance. It was generally agreed that backbiting and gossiping behind Wendy's back would merely accentuate the overall problem. Ground rules were therefore established and the team worked on ways of generalizing these ground rules for the day and how they might be applied to the team's functioning overall in the longer term, including areas such as respecting confidentiality, dealing with issues openly, not making personal attacks, and developing strong respect and support. It was agreed these should become the ground rules for the team generally. The team also identified some ambiguity about Wendy's role, vis-à-vis the role of the team leader. It was decided that this should be addressed in separate meetings between team members, the team leader, and Wendy herself in order to clarify her role and draw on her strengths and skills so that she could be more supportive to team members. Team members agreed to set up a time also to brief Wendy fully on the work of the day and to outline suggested solutions.

Sometimes the problem need not concern internal team functioning. One team I worked with was responsible for the production of springs used by the Ford motor company. They were experiencing problems with rejection rates from Ford, who informed them that the quality of their springs was not up to the standards required. A team meeting was set up to learn techniques of total quality management and continuous improvement from an expert. This led to changes in team objectives, strategies, and processes which had a dramatic impact on quality. The team was subsequently promoted far up the list of Ford's accredited suppliers.

Identifying what the problems are

Here the intervention focuses on the diagnosis of task-related problems. After the agreed identification of the nature of specific problems the team goes on to use appropriate strategies to overcome them in future.

When a team is functioning ineffectively, but it is unclear what is causing the problem, three alternatives are possible. The first involves group discussions to explore and clarify the nature of the problems. As indicated earlier, the amount of time spent exploring and clarifying problems is disproportionately more valuable than the time spent trying to solve them. Extended group discussions examining problem areas can lead to good problem identification. A second alternative is for team members to offer their ideas individually and privately about the nature of the problem in response to open-ended questions on short questionnaires. The third approach is to employ the Team Climate Inventory (a questionnaire measure for examining team functioning – see Anderson & West, 1998; the measure is published by ASE, Chiswick, London, www.ase-solutions.co.uk). This questionnaire, which has been used by many thousands of teams, is well validated and has excellent reliability. It can be used effectively as a diagnostic instrument to identify problems in team functioning and as an aid to identifying techniques associated with particular team problems. All members of a team should complete the questionnaire if the exercise is to be effective.

Social process interventions

Social interventions focus on interpersonal relationships, social support, team climate, support for growth and development of team members, and conflict resolution. They aim to promote a positive social climate and team member well-being.

Team social process interventions should be employed where a team has unsatisfactory answers to one or more of the questions listed in Exercise 4.1. Interventions should focus on one area rather than attempting to accomplish change in all. If, for example, the main problem is a lack of social support in the team, one solution might be to train team members in simple cocounselling techniques where individuals undertake to give a partner in the team a set period of time – say half an hour or an hour every month – to discuss work-related problems. It is a mutual contract where both team members are provided with equal time at the same session and ensures that all team members get regular support. The basic techniques of cocounselling can be taught at an intervention or on a course.

Exercise 4.1: Satisfaction with team social processes

	Yes, very definitely	Yes, but only somewhat	No, definitely not
Does the team provide adequate levels of social support for its members?	1	2	3
Does the team have constructive healthy approaches to conflict resolution?	1	2	3
Does the team have a generally warm and positive social climate?	1	2	3
Does the team provide adequate support for skill development, training, and personal development of all its members?	1	2	3

Have the whole team discuss team scores on this questionnaire and discuss whether there is a need to improve any of those areas of team social functioning.

If the problem relates more to support for growth and development the team might spend a day identifying each other's skill, training or personal development needs and then devise an action plan for how they could best provide the support to enable these needs to be met. General social climate problems can be addressed by asking team members to agree to simple behavioral rules for improving team functioning, such as arranging regular and varied social events. Again action planning and agreed contracting arrangements within the team can promote the likelihood that good intentions will be carried through. Finally, if the problem relates to a failure to resolve conflicts in a timely fashion, conflict resolution techniques based on the principles of assertiveness and ethical negotiation can be introduced (De Dreu & Van de Vliert, 1997; Fisher, Ury, & Patton, 1999).

◆ Role Clarification and Negotiation

One potential problem in teams is lack of clarity about team roles. To address this, team members can undertake the exercise in role clarification and negotiation (Exercise 4.2).

Exercise 4.2: Role negotiation exercise

Team members use mutual influence and negotiation in order to change team behaviors and improve team functioning.

Step 1
Each team member lists his or her objectives and principle activities on a piece of flip chart paper.

Step 2
Each piece of flip chart paper is hung on the wall around the room and team members examine each role.

Step 3
Under three headings on a piece of paper, each team member writes down what behaviors they would like that person to *do less*, *do more*, or *maintain at the present level* in their working relationship. For example, a personal assistant or receptionist might

Exercise 4.2: (cont'd)

indicate that he or she wants the senior manager they work with to keep them informed more fully of plans for the coming month, in order that they are up to date with the manager's movements. The receptionist may ask the manager not to check so often that paperwork has been completed, since it feels like controlling rather than trusting their role. He or she may also ask the manager to sustain these attempts to improve communication and to involve the personal assistant by seeking his or her views concerning the manager's work where appropriate.

Each person signs their name after their requests for more, less, or maintained behavior.

Step 4

Pairs of individuals within the team then meet to examine the end result. The two negotiate together in order to reach agreement about the various requests. This is a highly participative step in the exercise and some teams may need help in managing the negotiation, especially if a particular pair is having difficulty reaching agreement.

Through role negotiation, the needs of individuals are met more effectively and the functioning of individual members is dovetailed more into the objectives and needs of the team as a whole. This is a very powerful exercise which can enhance team functioning considerably, overcoming many of the problems of process loss and coordination described in chapter 1.

Conclusions

The blanket approach to team building employed in many organizations is unlikely to be effective for most teams. Those wanting to intervene in teams should ask "What intervention is most appropriate, for which teams, and at which point in time?" Then the following checklist can be used to ensure the appropriate focus for the intervention:

1   Are the objectives of the intervention clear?
2   Is the intervention appropriate for the particular issues facing the team?

3   Is the intervention appropriately timed?
4   Does the intervention attempt to cover too many areas?
5   Are means for sustaining change built in to the intervention?
6   Are facilitators employed who have the knowledge and skills
     required to conduct team-building interventions?
7   Will clear action plans emerge as a result of the team-building
     intervention?
8   Will regular reviews be instituted as a result of the team-building
     intervention?

This chapter has emphasized the need for teams to review their
functioning on a regular basis. Where a team is low in task reflexivity
it is necessary to address this failure of adaptability. Some fear that
such questioning generates conflict and uncertainty about the team's
direction. It is important to reassure team members that such reflexivity holds within it the seed of opportunity and greater effectiveness
that can produce an enhanced sense of competence, confidence, and
greater aspirations among team members. Moreover, the research evidence on reflexivity has strongly suggested that teams that do reflect on
strategies in this way are highly effective in long-term performance
(West, 2000). Reflexivity should therefore not simply occur during
team-building interventions; it should be part of the texture of the
day-to-day life of the team.

key revision points:

■ What is team building?

■ Does team building work?

■ What are the main types of team-building interventions?

■ When would you use them and why?

■ How would you go about designing a team-building
  intervention for a team you work in based on the
  material presented in this chapter?

FURTHER READING

Guzzo, R. A. (1996). Fundamental considerations about work groups. In M. A. West (ed.), *The Handbook of work group psychology* (pp. 3–23). Chichester, UK: John Wiley.

Guzzo, R. A. & Shea, G. P. (1992). Group performance and intergroup relations. In M. D. Dunnette and L. M. Hough (eds.), *Handbook of industrial and organizational psychology* (2nd edn, pp. 269–313). Palo Alto, CA: Consulting Psychologists Press.

Tannenbaum, S. I., Salas, E., & Cannon-Bowers, J. A. (1996). Promoting team effectiveness. In M. A. West (ed.), *The handbook of work group psychology* (pp. 503–29). Chichester, UK: Wiley.

◆ chapter five

Team Vision

Whatever you can do, or dream you can, begin it. Boldness
has genius, power and magic in it. Begin it now.

(Goethe)

key learning points:

■ Defining team vision, mission, objectives, goals, and
action plans

■ Why vision and objectives are central to team
effectiveness

■ The key dimensions and elements of team vision

■ Developing a team vision

■ Defining and developing a team strategy

◆ Defining Team Vision

The overriding reason why people work in teams is because they
share a common goal or purpose which they believe will be achieved
more successfully if they work together than if they work individually. This notion of shared purpose or shared vision is the defining
element of teams at work. By taking the time to clearly define team
vision, purpose, and objectives, those who work within teams have a
greater chance of being effective and creative in their work (Pritchard,
Jones, Roth, Stuebing, & Ekeberg, 1988; Tubbs, 1986).

Confusion surrounds the use of words such as "vision," "mission
statement," "objectives," and "goals." A useful way of thinking about
the meaning of these notions is to see them as parts of a tree (see

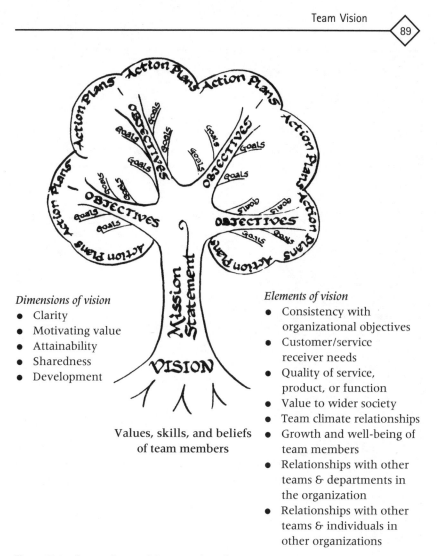

Dimensions of vision
- Clarity
- Motivating value
- Attainability
- Sharedness
- Development

Values, skills, and beliefs
of team members

Elements of vision
- Consistency with organizational objectives
- Customer/service receiver needs
- Quality of service, product, or function
- Value to wider society
- Team climate relationships
- Growth and well-being of team members
- Relationships with other teams & departments in the organization
- Relationships with other teams & individuals in other organizations

Figure 5.1 From value to vision to action plans

Figure 5.1). Vision represents the base of the tree growing from its roots in the values, skills, and beliefs of those within the team. The mission statement or trunk is the observable statement of the team's purpose. The team objectives are then the main branches of the tree which produce the goals (the twigs). Finally, the action plans for achieving goals can be seen as the leaves or foliage giving the tree its color.

An example will illustrate the difference between the concepts. Consider the vision of the Springwood primary health care team:

Team Vision: Springwood Primary Health Care Team

❑ *To give patients responsibility for their health and to make health promotion our primary orientation rather than illness treatment. We are also committed to collaborative working together with patients, each other, and the community. We place great emphasis on holistic approaches to health and the growth and well-being of our patients. We have a fundamental commitment to excellence in primary health care with the aim of improving the quality of life for the whole community. This vision is based on our shared values of:*

- *respect for other human beings;*
- *cooperation to achieve shared goals;*
- *the importance of freedom of choice for all individuals;*
- *the importance of equality of treatment and opportunity for all within our primary health care catchment area;*
- *commitment to effectiveness and excellence in our work, with the overall aim of improving the quality of life of our patients, those in the community, and of all those who work in this practice.*

This vision of the primary health care team sets out the principal values that underlie and drive the work of the team. It also indicates the degree of cohesion between the various aspects of the vision statement and represents an ideal for which to aim.

The mission statement of the team

❑ *"Our mission is to promote the health, growth, and well-being of all of those in our community, including patients, relatives, community members, and practice members by respecting the individual, encouraging cooperation and collaboration, and emphasizing excellence in all we do."*

This mission statement provides a short motivating set of words, summarizing and encapsulating the principle elements of the team's vision. It serves as a daily reminder to those who work in or with the team of the kinds of orientations that are expected in their joint working. It is a motivating symbol, helping the team to achieve its overall aims, and to make important choices at times when there is uncertainty about a decision. It provides a clear pointer to the directions the team should take when presented with alternative ways forward, or when presented with difficult decisions about the team's work.

Team objectives

❑ *Springwood defined the following objectives as a result of articulating its vision statement:*

1 *Increase the participation of patients in all aspects of the Springwood primary health care practice.*
2 *Emphasize health promotion as much as illness treatment in work with patients.*
3 *Involve all those who work in the practice in setting goals and in decision making.*
4 *Promote the growth and well-being of practice members.*
5 *Improve health care in the Springwood community.*
6 *Aim for excellence in all of our practice activities.*
7 *Develop greater knowledge of holistic and alternative approaches to health care in the community.*

These objectives are derived directly from the vision of the team and from its mission statement. They describe clearly the overall aims that team members have for the practice's work.

In order to illustrate the goals of the practice and how they are derived from objectives, consider the goals relating to objective 3:

Example: Objective 3 (above)

❑ *Involve all those who work in the practice in setting goals and in decision making.*

Goals to encourage group participation

1 *To encourage receptionists, district nurses, health visitors, practice nurses, practice manager, and other staff to participate in staff meetings.*
2 *To encourage all staff members to input their views on the goals of the practice.*

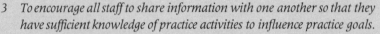

3   *To encourage all staff to share information with one another so that they have sufficient knowledge of practice activities to influence practice goals.*
4   *To encourage all staff to interact regularly in order to encourage joint influence over the activities of the practice.*
5   *To encourage all staff members to make their views known in order that they can have some influence over decisions that are made in the team.*

These goals can then be translated directly into the leaves of the tree as action plans. Action plans constitute specific actions to be taken in order to achieve the goals that will help toward the achievement of objectives. For example, in relation to goal 1 (above) of encouraging all of those involved in the practice to take part in meetings, Springwood created the following action plan:

❑   **Action plan**

Objective 3, goal 1 (as above)

1   *Weekly meetings will be held every Tuesday afternoon from 2.30 pm – 4.00 pm prior to the afternoon surgery. All staff are encouraged to attend. The agenda for the meeting and notification of the meeting will be circulated by the practice manager 24 hours beforehand.*
2   *Every six months the practice manager will set up a full one-day meeting where the team reviews its objectives, strategies, and processes at a congenial location, to be chaired by a facilitator. All members of staff are encouraged to attend this meeting and to make their views known about the practice's work. On this day, locums will be appointed to ensure that the practice's work is covered.*

From the vision grows a solid mission statement from which can be derived the principal objectives of the team. These guide the development of more detailed goals, which translate into action plans. In turn they should prompt specific actions by team members. Articulating the vision provides the basis for all of the team's activities. Surprisingly, few teams take the time out to work out their vision, mission statement, objectives, goals, and action plans. Yet considerable research reveals that planning makes it much more likely that action will ensue (Gollwitzer & Bargh, 1996).

➢   **Vision is a shared idea of a valued outcome that provides the motivation for the team's work.**

◆ The Dimensions of Team Vision

In order to develop a statement of team vision, a number of dimensions must be considered. These should include its clarity, motivating value, attainability, the extent to which it is shared by team members, and its ongoing development. Each of these dimensions is described below.

Clarity

In order for a team to determine its objectives, goals, and actions it must have a clear vision. If team members are unsure of what the shared orientations, values, and purposes of their colleagues are, it is difficult for them to articulate a clear statement that encapsulates these orientations and values. This requires that team members communicate about their work values and orientations. They must then find a form of words that expresses accurately and clearly these shared values, interests, and motivations. Later in this chapter the steps in fashioning a clear statement of vision are described.

Motivating value

The values that we bring to our work influence the effort we put into it. Consequently, for a team to work well together, team members must have some shared sense of the value of their work. For example, in health care settings people do work that accords with a basic value of helping others. To the extent that the vision reflects the underlying values of the team it is likely to motivate team loyalty, effort, and commitment (Locke, 1990; Locke, Shaw, Saari, & Latham, 1981; Locke & Latham, 1991).

In other settings it may not be so easy to engage people's values in the organizational objectives of the team. However, values about excellence in work, respect for individuals, and the growth and well-being of team members can be expressed within almost any context. For example, a team engaged in collecting financial debts may value treating all individuals with respect and consideration. It may also decide that team member skills should be enhanced and developed in order to encourage greater excellence both in team working and in relationships with others. Working in teams where the vision or values are inconsistent with one's own can create difficulties. For example, within a team in a personnel department that is being directed to appoint people on contracts offering little job security, poor pay, and poor career development opportunities, team members may work less hard simply because the approach is inconsistent with their values. Many people experience working in situations where they feel that the work that they are required to do is in conflict with their core values. The consequence is that we work less hard or look for alternative jobs – we are less motivated and less committed.

Attainability

"That man is truly free who desires what he is able to perform, and does what he desires." (Rousseau)

When a team is set unattainable goals it can have a demotivating effect. It may also lead to some of the problems described in the last chapter, such as free-riding and social loafing. Consequently team members' commitment and motivation may be substantially reduced. This depends to some extent upon the nature of the task they are being asked to perform. A top management team at OXFAM may be less demotivated by the difficulty of achieving food for all by the year 2010, simply because of the enormous motivating value of the vision of the team. There is, therefore, a trade-off between attainability and the motivating value of a team's vision.

Sharedness

The vision should also be shared and this is partly itself dependent upon the extent to which the vision is negotiated. Where team members feel they have made a real contribution to the determination of the vision and that, more importantly, it is in accord with their personal values, they will be more motivated and committed to its achievement (Latham & Yukl, 1975, 1976).

Ability to develop

A danger of team working is that decisions about vision made at one point in time become cast in stone. Because teams are constantly evolving – the people within the teams are changing their views, developing new skills, and changing values – it is important that the vision of the team evolves in the same way. Similarly, the environment within which the team operates goes through change; organizations change strategies and society changes its views. There is more emphasis now on flexible patterns of working and on environmental protection and equal opportunities. Teams that formerly might not have considered these issues may now need to give them careful consideration. Consequently a team's vision must be regularly reviewed in order to ensure that it is alive, evolving, up-to-date, and representative of the changing values and orientations of team members. Otherwise, team vision can become a straitjacket within which the team is prevented from developing in new directions.

◆ The Elements of Team Vision

It is possible to consider eight major elements of team vision which are the areas upon which a team's vision may focus:

1 *Consistency with organizational objectives*
In some circumstances a team may decide that it is important for its own values, purposes, and orientations to act as a minority group that aims to bring about change in organizational objectives. For example, within the UK National Health Service there has been considerable debate about the conflict that exists between providing health care and reducing spending. Some teams have attempted to subvert the second orientation where they see it as conflicting with their aim of providing quality health care for all. So, in some circumstances, a team may work effectively when its vision contradicts stated organizational objectives. However, it is very important that teams are clear about when they wish to act as minority groups in order that they may develop appropriate strategies to bring about the kinds of organizational change they wish. This is an issue discussed in more depth in Chapter 11.

2 *Customer/service receiver needs*
To what extent will the team work to provide excellence in service to its customers, whether they be customers within or outside the organization? To what extent are service receivers seen as people who are to be merely satisfied, rather than people who are to receive the best quality of service available? For example, a teaching team in a university department might prefer to emphasize research excellence above the quality of teaching provided to students. Alternatively, they

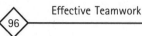
may strive to admit as many students as possible, putting pedagogical excellence second. A car maintenance team may emphasize satisfying the customer above ever-increasing profitability (though these two may not necessarily contradict one another).

3 *Quality of product, service, or function*
A major emphasis within organizations is the quality of services and functioning within organizational settings. Team members may also discuss the extent to which top quality will characterize their own working relationships. This may be reflected in the speed with which requests for information within the team are met, and also the quality of information that is eventually produced.

4 *Value to wider society*
It is unusual for teams to take time out to consider the value of their work for the wider society. Consideration of this, and ways in which it can be enhanced, is an important way of encouraging both team cohesion and greater team effectiveness. Such consideration may promote conflict if team members perceive their work to be irrelevant to the wider society or if there are conflicts between team members about the potential value of the team's work. However, throughout this book it is argued that such conflict enables team members to achieve clear perception of the purposes of their work and therefore enhances team effectiveness and creativity.

5 *Team climate relationships*
Team climate relationships are often neglected when teams discuss their functioning. If team members have such difficult relationships that members are inclined to leave the team, long-term team viability is threatened. Teams therefore need to consider the type of team climate they wish to create. Team climate refers to aspects of teamwork such as warmth, humor, amount of conflict, mutual support, sharing, backbiting, emphasis of status, participation, information sharing, level of criticism of each other's work, and support for new ideas. Chapters 6 to 10 consider various ways in which the team climate can be enhanced.

6 *Growth and well-being of team members*
Another element of vision is support for the skill development and well-being of team members. Growth, skill development, and challenge are central elements of work life and teams can be a major source of support. They may provide opportunities for skill sharing and support for new training. One issue is the extent to which team members will support skill development and training that may further

someone's career, although this may not contribute immediately to team effectiveness.

Another area of concern for a team is the general well-being of its members. This is especially true for those working in conditions of high stress, such as caring professionals. The social support that team members provide can have a buffering effect, preventing stress-related illnesses.

7 *Relationships with other teams and departments in the organization*
Teams rarely operate in isolation. They interact with other teams and departments within the organization, for example, in cooperating in cross-functional teams or competing for scarce resources. Therefore teams need to decide what orientation – cooperation or competition – they will adopt toward other teams and departments within their organization.

Groups often compete as a result of "group identification," where people tend to favor their own group and discriminate against other groups, leading to destructive working relationships (see chapter 11). For example, nurses working in community health settings may find themselves in conflict with doctors. Equally, they may find themselves cooperating closely and working effectively with other professionals such as social workers. Those groups that are most successful build cooperative relationships with the other teams or departments with whom they interact in the course of their work.

8 *Relationships with teams outside the organization*
Similar issues arise in considering team relationships with other organizations. For example, BBC TV Continuing Education production teams are concerned with issues that affect the whole community. In producing programs about how families can function most effectively, they may therefore want to work closely with the relevant voluntary and professional organizations. On the other hand, a team may decide to take a very critical orientation to the work of these organizations and may wish to distance itself in the making of a program. In order for a team to have a clear shared vision about its work, it must make explicit (where relevant) the quality and nature of relationships it seeks with organizations and individuals.

◆ Strategy for Teams

Strategy is a word that is sprinkled in organizational conversations and documents like confetti at a wedding. But what does it mean in practice? If a team wishes to determine a strategy, how does it do so? A way of designing strategy is to separate out the elements that together make up strategy: they are domains, vehicles, differentiators, economic logic, and sequencing and stages. Each of these is explained below with an example from a business consultancy team (Aston Organization Development, www.astonOD.ac.uk), developed from the work of a university work psychology department.

Domains

Domains are the content of teams' activities and the products or services they offer. In the case of Aston Organization Development (AOD), this includes consultancy to organizations that wish to introduce team-based working; products in the form of manuals, guides, and test instruments that help with the introduction of team-based working; consultancy to organizations that wish to promote innovation and creativity; and products including test instruments to assess levels of creativity and innovation in organizations, as well as instruments to assess the supportiveness of the environment for innovation

Vehicles

Vehicles include the means by which these products and services will be developed and delivered, including people, marketing, partnerships, and contacts. AOD identified the vehicles as the principal consultants in the business (mostly work psychologists), and associated consultants (skilled colleagues not employed by AOD but known to the principal consultants as competent practitioners who would welcome additional work). AOD also saw their extensive networks of contacts with senior managers and HR directors in organizations as important vehicles for their work, since these contacts potentially offered important business opportunities.

Differentiators

What differentiates the team's work and makes it unique and identifiable? This is an important question to answer since it relates to the commercial value of the team's work as well as to valued identity for team members. Why would people remember the team unless there were aspects of its work that differentiated it from others? AOD recognized that the academic reputation of its principal consultants and their research expertise and credentials made the team stand out from consultancies in general. This was a consultancy whose work was supported by a solid research base. Moreover, their focus on team-based working was unusual since very few, if any, consultancies offered a service designed to help with introducing organization-wide team-based working.

Economic logic

How will the team ensure that it is funded to do its work and that there are sufficient resources to implement the elements of the strategy? Any team has to ensure that the economic logic for its strategy is worked out and articulated. AOD identified earnings from consultancy during its early phases as a source of income that would allow it to slowly develop web- and CD-based instruments that could be sold commercially and that would potentially be a major income source. Public speaking by two of the best-known consultants would also ensure a steady income stream in the first year. Finally, the AOD team identified the value of developing booklets that managers could use for practical advice on developing creativity and innovation in organizations, on conducting research in organizations, and for managing change. These would have mass market appeal for managers at all levels and would provide another income stream in the first years of the company's operation.

Sequences and stages

Strategies need to have time plans that are realistic and do not require team members to try to accomplish too many tasks all at the same time. In what order and with what duration will plans be put into effect? AOD decided that for the first two to three years the principal focus would be on delivering large-scale consultancy support to organizations requiring help to introduce team-based working and encourage creativity and innovation. An intermediate step (two to four years) would be the development of booklets and first examples of web-based questionnaire instruments that organizations could use to assess aspects of functioning. Licencing of users of instruments and high profile marketing would be the final stage of the team's five-year strategy.

By thinking through these five elements of strategy, teams can articulate a strategy that enables them to chart their directions and activities for the future. The vision provides the destination; the strategy provides the means for getting to the destination.

This chapter began by emphasizing the fundamental importance of team vision for effective team working. This is because without a clear beacon to guide it the team can often be diverted from its course by organizational demands, the changing interests of team members, or other external pressures. With a clear sense of vision, rooted in the shared values of members, and a practical and thoroughly developed strategy, the team will maintain a good course toward its valued aims and objectives.

key revision points:

- What are the differences between team vision, mission, and objectives?

- How would you develop a team vision for a team you know well?

- What are the dimensions and elements of team vision?

- What are the elements of a team strategy?

- Design a strategy for a team you know well.

- What is the difference between team vision and team strategy?

FURTHER READING

Gollwitzer, P. M. & Bargh, J. A. (eds.) (1996). *The psychology of action: Linking cognition and motivation to behavior*. New York: The Guilford Press.

Latham, G. P. & Locke, E. A. (1991). Self-regulation through goal setting. *Organizational Behavior and Human Decision Processes, 50,* 212–47.

Locke, E. & Latham, G. (1991). *A theory of goal setting and task motivation*. Englewood Cliffs, NJ: Prentice-Hall.

Poulton, B. C. & West, M. A. (1994). Primary health care team effectiveness: Developing a constituency approach. *Health and Social Care, 2,* 77–84.

Pritchard, R. D., Jones, S. D., Roth, P. L., Stuebing, K. K., & Ekeberg, S. E. (1988). Effects of group feedback, goal setting, and incentives on organizational productivity. *Journal of Applied Psychology, 73,* 337–58.

Tubbs, M. E. (1986). Goal setting: A meta-analytic examination of the empirical evidence. *Journal of Applied Psychology, 71,* 474–83.

chapter six

Being Part of a Team

Difference of opinion leads to enquiry and enquiry to truth.
(Thomas Jefferson)

key learning points:

- Team interaction frequency and team performance
- Information sharing in teams
- Barriers to team decision making
- How to improve team decision making
- How to build a sense of safety in teams

We create teams in order to utilize the skills, knowledge, and abilities of people who make up the team in ways that ensure their collective efforts enable them to accomplish tasks they could not manage alone. To be in a team means to participate fully, and to lead a team means encouraging team members to meet together, share information and ideas, and debate fully and intelligently the best way of accomplishing the task or providing services for customers or clients. In short, teamwork is about participation. Being part of a team means taking responsibility for team objectives, team strategies, and team processes. While team work implies differentiation of roles and responsibilities and thereby that people will take leadership positions, this does not mean that the team leader is solely responsible for determining team objectives, strategies, processes, and outcomes. On the contrary, in effective work teams, all team members are aware of and sensitive to team functioning.

◆ The Elements of Team Participation

Being part of a team involves participating, which includes interacting, information sharing, influencing decision making, and creating a sense of safety.

Interaction

In order for a group of individuals who share a common goal to be called a team they must have some minimal ongoing interaction, otherwise their efforts are essentially uncoordinated and unaggregated. Teams interact during task performance and socially; both are equally important. Social interactions might include parties, lunches, or informal chats in the corridors to discuss family matters or sporting events. These interactions strengthen the social bonding, cohesion, and familiarity that enable people to feel safe with one another. Interaction during task performance provides an exchange of information, communication, and so forth, which enables the team to coordinate individual member efforts to achieve their shared goals. In effect they learn to dance the dance of teamwork better, the more time they spend dancing together. Imagine the success of a football team that only met to play together once or twice a year compared with a team that played together and discussed their performance every week.

Case study: Team interaction

I was once asked to act as a facilitator for a team that provided consultancy services to a large organization. On the first day the team emphasized how effective they were as a team. But after an hour or two of interaction the team had split into two opposing groups in separate rooms, accompanied by strong expressions of anger and hostility. It emerged that the team had not met together for over 18 months and had assumed they shared similar orientations and objectives in their work. In fact, team members were working at cross purposes and, even after two days together, there was still some tension over their differing orientations to the work. This seemed to be due to the surprise of discovering these differences rather than to any intrinsic incompatibility in their work orientations.

What this case suggests is that interaction and meetings are vital for team functioning. Without regular meetings, both formal and informal, important information is not exchanged and assumptions and expectations may be built up that are not matched by reality. Indeed our research results reveal that even poor team meetings are better than no team meetings at all, since members get to exchange information in small informal dyads or groups before, after, and even during meetings (Borrill, West, Shapiro, & Rees, 2000). Team members may begin to diverge in their views about what is important for the team, and perceptions of other team members' actions may be incorrect. Misapprehension and misunderstanding can lead to conflict and lack of coordination in terms of task processes. These in turn lead to lowered team effectiveness.

It is not possible to specify an ideal frequency of interaction. Some teams will need to meet more often than others and meetings between some team members will need to be more frequent than between other team members. Teams should meet *minimally* once a month, in order to update one another on developments. Every six months too, it is valuable for teams to take time out (a day or two days) to reflect upon and modify as necessary their objectives, their strategies for achieving those objectives, and team processes such as communication and the participation in decision making.

Chairing meetings

- Arrange meetings with a clear agenda. Specify the start time and end time in advance. Establish a norm of team members arriving on time. Hold the meeting in a location that is comfortable (e.g., has windows), has appropriate equipment (e.g., flip charts, overhead projector). Chair the meeting yourself (rotating chairs are a misguided attempt at democracy) or have a team member who is an effective chair do the job. Stick to the agenda unless absolutely necessary and work out rough timings for topics beforehand.

- Encourage everyone who may have a view to share their views. Exploring ideas is helpful in decision making and the meeting will usually be more productive (and quicker) than if you suppress discussion. Ensure everyone is contributing during the meeting. Use a variety of ways of encouraging discussion (have people discuss in pairs and small groups and report back). Summarize frequently.

- Once views have been expressed and opinions discussed move efficiently toward a decision. Don't defer decisions unless it is necessary, avoid passing decisions on to other meetings (unless you don't have the information) and setting up subgroups for more meetings.

- Keep control of the meeting and maintain positive feelings by being optimistic, warm, polite, enthusiastic, and committed to the work of the meeting. Acknowledge and thank people for their contributions. Take time out if things become heated.
- Review the usefulness of meetings on a regular basis and discuss how they could be improved.

Box 6.1: Ground rules for team meetings

Everyone takes responsibility for:

- keeping us on track if we get off;
- facilitating group input, not just your own;
- raising questions about procedures (e.g., asking the group to clarify where it is going and offering summaries of the issues being discussed to make sure we have a shared understanding of them);
- using good listening skills: either build on the ongoing discussion or clearly signal that we want to change the subject and ask if that is OK.

TEAMWORK IN PRACTICE

Information sharing

Information in a team context is data that alters the understanding of the team as a whole and/or of individual team members. Monitoring information is essential for team effectiveness.

Information can be rich or poor to the extent that it alters understanding, that is, the more it alters understanding the richer it is. For example, in a changeover of teams in a chemical processing plant, information relating to potentially volatile reactions noted during the previous shift is rich information. It communicates the likelihood of risk to the team taking over. On the other hand, a computer printout of the number of visits to children under five years of age made by a nurse during the course of one month may communicate relatively little information to the nurse's supervisor, since it provides no indication of the difficulty of the visits or the quality of the work.

The medium of transfer of information is determined by its richness. The least rich information is transferred by paper or email messages. Slightly richer information is given in the form of telephone conversations or video conferencing, but information is most richly transferred when people talk face to face. Voice inflection, facial expression, body posture, and gestures all add to the richness of information transfer. Moreover, in face-to-face meetings it is possible to ask questions and explore issues in depth. In general, use print and email to exchange information, communicate news, and ask questions, and always use face-to-face meetings to express concerns, complaints, and find resolutions to conflicts. It is irresponsible to use email to attack, harangue, or abuse others.

Within team settings the ideal medium is face to face, except for routine messages. Of course, there is a temptation to avoid such direct communication since this may take up time. In general teams err on the side of email messages and communicate too little face to face. Yet the whole basis of team work is communication, coordination, cooperation, and transfer of information in the richest possible form. Consequently there is a real need for team members to address issues about information sharing and communication and to examine the media that they use to transfer this information.

Increasingly, individuals find themselves working within dispersed teams, often with colleagues who live in different countries or in other situations that provide little opportunity for informal or regular communication. Such teams need formal regular communication and meetings where there are opportunities to chat informally or socialize to help increase cohesion and trust. An international computer company that has outlawed "personal chat" via email may have saved a minimal amount on telephone charges, but they have lost a great deal more through the reinforcement of already pervasive divisions within their international teams.

Virtual teams (e.g., of members distributed across several European countries), that rely on email, video conferencing, and telephone conferences are less effective and innovative than teams that are colocated (Agarwal, 2003). The richness of information transfer and the learning about teamwork are simply much greater among those working in colocated or face-to-face teams. Consequently virtual teams must work much harder to communicate effectively. At a minimum they should meet for some days prior to starting work together to agree team objectives, strategies, and decision-making and communication processes. Because we human beings are hard-wired to read information from faces, the loss of that information source in virtual teams inevitably means they are less effective than they would otherwise be.

Case study: Manufacturing success

Information flows vary enormously, depending upon the organizational settings. On a visit to an innovative manufacturing company in Scotland, I met the personnel director who had previously worked in the Civil Service. He told me that it took him a year of working in the manufacturing company to receive the number of written memoranda that he normally received in a week within the Civil Service. Another change was a much higher level of face-to-face communication in the manufacturing company, which led to a much richer understanding. The company was characterized by enormous flexibility, few rules and regulations, and a high degree of innovativeness.

Exercise 6.1: Information sharing in the team

What information do you currently receive from each team member?

Name of team member	Content of information received	Current medium (face-to-face, email)	Current frequency (hourly, daily, weekly
1			
2			
3			
4			
5			
6			
7			
8			

Exercise 6.1: (cont'd)

What information would you like from each team member?

Name of team member	Content of information desired	Desired medium	Desired frequency
1			
2			
3			
4			
5			
6			
7			
8			

Team Decision Making

A principle assumption behind the structuring of organizational functioning into work teams is that teams will make better decisions than individual team members working alone. A good deal of research has shown that teams are subject to social processes that undermine their decision-making effectiveness. While teams tend to make decisions that are better than the average of decisions made by individual members, they may consistently fall short of the quality of decisions made by the best individual member. The implications of this for the functioning of boards and senior executive teams are considerable. Organizational behaviorists and social psychologists have therefore devoted considerable effort to identifying the social processes that create deficiencies in team decision making:

1 *Team members must take into account some of the hidden dangers of team decision making.* One is the powerful tendency for team members to focus on information that all team members share before the discussion starts and to ignore new information that only one or two

team members know about. Even when they introduce this information, team members are likely to ignore it since it is not information they all already share. Psychologists call this the *hidden profile* phenomenon and teams can avoid it by ensuring that members have clearly defined roles so that each is seen as a source of potentially unique and important information, that members listen carefully to colleagues' contributions in decision making, and that leaders alert the team to information that is uniquely held by only one or two members (Stasser & Stewart, 1992).

2   *Personality factors* can affect social behavior in various ways. For example, any shyness by individual members, who may be hesitant to offer their opinions and knowledge assertively, will mean that they fail to contribute fully to the team's store of knowledge (Barrick, Stewart, Neubert, & Mount, 1998).

3   Team members are subject to *social conformity* effects causing them to withhold opinions and information contrary to the majority view – especially an organizationally dominant view (Brown, 2000).

4   Team members may lack *communication skills* and so be unable to present their views and knowledge successfully. The person who has mastered impression management within the organization may disproportionately influence team decisions even in the absence of expertise.

5   The team may be *dominated* by particular individuals who take up disproportionate "air time" or argue so vigorously with the opinion of others that their own views prevail. It is noteworthy that "air time" and expertise are correlated in high-performing teams and uncorrelated in teams that perform poorly.

6   Particular team members may be *egocentric* (such as senior organizational members whose egocentricity may have carried them to the top) and consequently unwilling to consider opinions or knowledge offered by other team members contrary to their own.

7   *Status and hierarchy* effects can cause some members' contributions to be valued and attended to disproportionately. When a senior executive is present in a meeting, his or her views are likely to have an undue influence on the outcome.

8   *Group polarization* refers to the tendency of work teams to make more extreme decisions than the average of individual members' opinions or decision. Team decisions tend to be either more risky or more conservative than the average of individuals members' opinions or decisions. Thus shifts in the extremity of decisions affecting the competitive strategy of an organization can occur simply as a result of team processes rather than for rational or well-judged reasons (Semin & Glendon, 1973; Walker & Main, 1973).

9   In his study of failures in policy decisions, social psychologist Irving Janis identified the phenomenon of *groupthink*, whereby tightly knit groups may err in their decision making because they are more concerned with achieving agreement than with the quality of the decisions made. This can be especially threatening to organizational functioning where different departments see themselves as competing with one another, promoting "in-group" favoritism and groupthink (see chapter 7).

10   The *social loafing effect* is the tendency of individuals in teams to work less hard than they do when individual contributions can be identified and evaluated. In organizations, individuals may put less effort into achieving quality decisions in meetings if they perceive that their contribution is hidden in overall team performance (Karau & Williams, 1993).

11   Diffusion of *responsibility* can inhibit individuals from taking responsibility for action when in the presence of others. People seem to assume that responsibility will be shouldered by others who are present in a situation requiring action. In organizational settings, individuals may fail to act in a crisis involving the functioning of expensive technology, assuming that others in their team are taking responsibility for taking necessary decisions. Consequently, the overall quality of team decisions is threatened (Latané & Darley, 1970).

12   The study of brainstorming groups shows that quantity and often quality of ideas produced by individuals working separately are consistently superior to those produced by a group working together. This is due to a *production-blocking* effect. Individuals are inhibited from both thinking of new ideas and offering them aloud to the group by the competing verbalizations of others (Diehl & Stroebe, 1987).

What role does the team leader play in decision making? There are many situations where teams need leaders. In moments of crisis there may not be time for the whole team to discuss the appropriate course of action in depth. One individual may be required to grasp the nettle and take decisions for the good of the whole team. In most circumstances, however, teams can sanction individuals to take the decision in specific areas of the team's activity. In order to achieve a balance between excessive democracy and authoritarianism, team reviews of decision-making processes should be conducted every six months to a year. The purpose of these reviews should be to determine which team members should take executive decisions on behalf of the team and in which areas.

◆ The Stepladder Technique for Decision Making

In order to overcome the problems of team decision making described above, Rogelberg and colleagues (Rogelberg, Barnes-Farrell, & Lowe, 1992) proposed a strategy called "the stepladder technique." This involves each member of the team presenting his or her views to the team without having heard the views of other team members first. The aim is to build a complete picture of the varied inputs of the team before they consider their collective problem interpretation or decision. This approach can be adapted given the widespread use of email. Each team member is given time to think through the particular problem or issue before sending a document to the team presenting his or her views. Each member emails his or her preliminary views about the appropriate course of action before viewing others' preliminary solutions. A final decision is delayed until all members of the team have had an opportunity to present their views and there has been a full and inclusive face-to-face discussion. This approach gives each member of the team time to reflect upon the particular problem in order to prepare his or her case, independent of other team members. It also gives time for some discussion to take place about all the presentations. Decision making is thus postponed until all team members have presented their views.

This approach to decision making facilitates communication, since all members of the team have an opportunity to present their views. Such communication leads to a greater number or range of ideas being presented since conformity processes are minimized. It also inhibits social loafing effects since individual accountability is emphasized and there is no opportunity for individual members to hide behind others' contributions. Furthermore, because each member is required to present his or her views without the benefit of having heard all the other team members' views, disagreements are more likely and therefore the quality of decision making and discussion may be improved. The team is exposed to the continual input of fresh ideas that have not been affected by team norms, and this may lead to a vigorous evaluation and exploration of contrasting ideas. Considerable evidence indicates that such exploration of divergent opinions within teams leads to better quality decision making (Tjosvold, 1998).

Another cause of poor decision making is what is called "satisficing" – the tendency to go with the first acceptable solution rather than to generate a range of solutions and then to select the best option. By delaying decision making until every team member has had an opportunity to present his or her views, the number of possible solutions or options available to the team is maximized (Lam & Schaubroeck, 2000).

A major deficiency of team decision making in experimental studies is the failure of teams to outperform their best individual member. Because the stepladder technique increases the likelihood of each individual member being heard, opportunities for the best individual member to display his or her expertise are increased considerably. This is important because recent research has shown that unless the best individual member happens to be assertive and dominant, he or she is unlikely to influence team ratings. Where expertise and "air time" are correlated, teams tend to perform well. In poor performing teams "air time" and expertise tend to be uncorrelated.

How effective is the stepladder technique? Research evidence indicates that there is no difference in the time taken for decision making between teams using the stepladder technique and conventional techniques. The quality of team decision scores is generally significantly better than in conventional teams. Moreover, more than half the stepladder teams exceed their best members' scores, compared with only one tenth of conventional teams.

These statistical findings tell one story, but the impressions of those in stepladder groups reveal further important information. Stepladder group members report feeling much less pressured to conform; tend to agree on the final group decision, perceive themselves as working unusually well together, and perceive the group as more friendly. They also see themselves as having worked harder on the task than do conventional group members. Moreover, there tends to be more questioning of views and ideas in stepladder groups than in conventional groups.

In effect, stepladder groups continually remake their decisions, and this has beneficial effects on team decision making. It is significant that the most productive members in stepladder groups report that they have more chance to say what they want (more so than any other group members), which suggests that the stepladder approach reveals knowledge and individual expertise to other group members. In other words, better ideas are not only more likely to be expressed, but are more likely to be attended to and recognized as better.

Exercise 6.2: A short form of the stepladder technique

1   Allow 10 minutes – all individuals within the team engage in analyzing the problem and coming up with potential problem solutions.
2   Allow 10 minutes – team members work in pairs to present and discuss their respective solutions separate from other team members.
3   Allow 10 minutes – two pairs of individuals present their solutions to each other and discuss the solutions. This process continues until the whole team comes together.
4   The whole team considers solutions presented, final discussions take place and a decision is made. About 40–60 minutes should be allowed for creating the one best solution for the problem.

The stepladder technique is a method of decision making that can overcome some of the problems of team decision making. By enabling members to participate fully, commitment, intrinsic interest, creativity and the input of all members' abilities, knowledge, and skills are increased.

Safety in Teams

It is a truism of human behavior that commitment and involvement are most likely to occur when people feel safe. Just as children who have strong and secure bonding with their parents are more likely to explore their surroundings more extensively (Ainsworth, 1982), so too are people in teams more likely to take risks in introducing new and improved ways of doing things if they feel they are unlikely to be attacked or denigrated by other team members. The child taken to the park by a parent will be more likely to leave the parent's side sooner and make longer forays into the park if he or she is securely bonded and attached to that parent. Where children have poor relationships with their parents, they are likely to hover anxiously close rather than explore their new surroundings. In therapy, clients are likely to explore threatening aspects of their own experience when they feel supported and safe from attack by their therapist. It is not for purely ideological reasons that Carl Rogers urged therapists to adopt an attitude of unconditional positive regard for patients. Such an orientation is likely to induce feelings of safety and thereby encourage greater exploration of difficult experiences.

Similarly in team settings, it is important that team members perceive a climate of interpersonal safety, free from the possibility of attack or threat. Where the team is perceived as unsafe, members behave cautiously and maintain a kind of anxious watchfulness in their work. For example, if team members in a customer service team feels they are being criticized constantly by colleagues, they will be unlikely to suggest new ways of providing customer services and offering ideas for improving team functioning. Individual members will also be unlikely to exercise their own initiative in improving the quality of support to customers. Each team member has a responsibility to promote safety. This involves encouraging others to offer their views and then supportively exploring those ideas. Trust in teams is vital to team members' preparedness to cooperate (Korsgaard, Brodt, & Sapienza, 2003).

In a revealing study on safety in teams, Edmondson (1996) found major differences between newly formed intensive care nursing teams in their management of medication errors. In some groups, members openly acknowledged and discussed their medication errors (giving too much or too little of a drug, or administering the wrong drug) and discussed ways to avoid their occurrence. In others, members kept information about errors to themselves. Learning about the causes of these errors as a team, and devising innovations to prevent future errors, were only possible in groups of the former type. In these groups there was a climate of safety developed partly by the leader. Edmondson gives an example of how, in one learning-oriented team, discussion of a recent error led to innovation in equipment. An intravenous medication pump was identified as a source of consistent errors and so was replaced by a different type of pump. She also gives the example of how failure to discuss errors and generate innovations led to costly failure in the Hubble telescope development project. Edmondson (1996, 1999) argues that learning and innovation will only take place where group members trust other members' intentions. Where this is the case, team members believe that well-intentioned action will not lead to punishment or rejection by the team. Edmondson argues that safety "is meant to suggest a realistic, learning oriented attitude about effort, error and change – not to imply a careless sense of permissiveness, nor an unrelentingly positive affect. Safety is not the same as comfort; in contrast, it is predicted to facilitate risk." (Edmondson, 1999, p. 14).

Box 6.2: Creating an atmosphere of trust, support, and safety

TEAMWORK IN PRACTICE

Team leaders can contribute to an atmosphere of trust, support, and safety in teams by encouraging members to feel excited, energetic, and enthusiastic about the work. If members of a team start to be distressed, mistrustful, and nervous, then the team climate will mirror this. To create trust leaders must also encourage team members to take risks and rely on each other. The best way they can do this is to model trust themselves. Leaders should specify clearly for the team what they are required to do and then trust them to find the best ways of achieving that (specify ends but not means). Leaders must provide team members with support when they want it of course, but must show clearly that they trust the team to do the job and do it well.

Leaders should encourage team members to take risks with each other too. We trust when we find we can take risks. Also it is valuable for leaders to emphasize that team members share the same fate; they must trust each other if they are to achieve the goal. By encouraging open and honest communication between team members, leaders can help team members to see that they share the same values in their work.

Where the team is perceived as unsafe, members behave cautiously and maintain a kind of anxious watchfulness in their work. For example, if a team member feels he or she is being criticized constantly by another team member, he or she will be less likely to suggest new and improved ways of doing things. Each of your team members has a responsibility to promote safety and this responsibility should be agreed early on.

But safety is not the same as comfort; it encourages risk. You should therefore build safety by encouraging support and discouraging threats between team members. If one team member makes others feel threatened, coach the person and deal with the problem effectively. Chronic anxiety and anger in your team not only undermine team safety, they also damage team members' health (Goleman, 1995). You can build safety by encouraging team members to accept each other, promoting humor, warmth, and support.

Safety is the affective context within which people are more likely to engage in effective team working based on trust, acceptance, humor, warmth, and support. Together these lead to the involvement, commitment, and creativity of team members in team functioning and equally important, to a positive climate that enhances the mental health of people at work. The next chapter examines what can go wrong in a team even when there are clear visions and objectives and high levels of participation.

key revision points:

- Why is team interaction so important?

- How often should teams meet?

- What are the main information media that teams use and that communicate information best?

- What are some of the main barriers to effective team decision making?

- How can they be overcome?

- How can we build a sense of psychological safety in teams?

FURTHER READING

Guzzo, R. & Salas, E. (eds.) (1995). *Team effectiveness and decision-making in organizations*. San Francisco, CA: Jossey-Bass.

Koslowski, S. W. J. & Bell, B. S. (2002). Work groups and teams in organizations. In W. C. Borman, D. R. Ilgen, & R. J. Klimoski (eds.), *Comprehensive handbook of psychology (vol. 12): Industrial and organizational psychology* (pp. 333–75). New York: Wiley.

March, J. G. (1994). *A primer on decision making*. New York: Free Press.

Weick, K. E. (1995). *Sense making in organizations*. Thousand Oaks, CA: Sage.

chapter seven

Aiming for Excellence in Team Work

The hottest places in hell are reserved for those who, in time of great moral crisis, maintain their neutrality.

(Dante)

Have you learned lessons only of those who admired you, and were tender with you and stood aside for you? Have you not learned great lessons from those who braced themselves against you, and disputed the passage with you?

(Walt Whitman)

key learning points:

- Conformity processes in teams and the dangers of "groupthink"

- Team defense mechanisms and how to overcome them

- The value of constructive controversy

- Techniques for encouraging team task focus

- Minority views and dissent in teams

Teams exist to get a job done or achieve a set of objectives. Their principle commitment should therefore be to doing that. In well-functioning teams, inevitably, that means team members will have many vigorous debates about how best to do the task. Ensuring the team has a task focus is the subject of this chapter.

So far, we have considered the importance of a clear vision or set of objectives along with high levels of participation in a team. However, these two elements are necessary but insufficient to guarantee effective team working. There is evidence that these very factors in isolation can be the seeds of disastrous outcomes. Consider the following account as an illustration of how clear objectives and high levels of participation and cohesion may lead to quite the opposite in the effectiveness of teamwork. In 1961, an aura of optimism, enthusiasm, and vigor surrounded the United States presidency. President Kennedy and his advisors were young, enthusiastic, and had captured the optimism of many Americans with their commitment to civil rights and democracy. However, at the beginning of the presidency, this group characterized by high levels of vision, cohesiveness, and participation was responsible for one of the major foreign policy fiascos of the decade. This was the support of the invasion of Cuba in the Bay of Pigs affair. Against much intelligence information that indicated the likely failure of such an adventure, Kennedy and his advisors authorized the CIA to support Cuban exiles in an invasion. The Cuban army easily repulsed the invasion, capturing or killing the exiles. Afterwards many commentators questioned how Kennedy and his advisors could have concluded that the adventure would have been successful.

 Groupthink

In a revealing analysis of the Bay of Pigs affair, Irving Janis (1982) came to the conclusion that a dangerous pattern of group processes was responsible. Janis argued that Kennedy's cabinet was prone to the detrimental effects of "groupthink." Groupthink arises where five conditions are present:

1   The team is a highly cohesive group of individuals who are more concerned with their own cohesiveness and unanimity than with quality of decision making.
2   The group typically insulates itself from information and opinions from outside and particularly those that go against the group view.
3   Members of the group rarely engage in any kind of systematic search through the available options for appropriate solutions, choosing instead to go with the first available option on which there is a consensus.
4   The group is under pressure to achieve a decision.
5   One individual dominates the group – this is a particularly important factor in the development of groupthink.

Each of the following is a symptom of groupthink:

- Where the conditions for groupthink exist, a cohesive group will exert strong pressures on dissenting individuals to conform to the view of the majority.
- The group has a shared illusion of unanimity and correctness. Dean Rusk, who was Kennedy's Secretary of State for Defense, described how there was a "curious atmosphere of assumed consensus" within the group.
- Members of the group ignore or dismiss cues that there may be dissent within the group. Indeed some members of the Kennedy cabinet later described how they had felt inhibited from offering ideas or views opposing the Bay of Pigs plan, even when they felt privately that there were major problems with it.
- Group members block information from outside the group. Bobby Kennedy (US Attorney General at the time) described how he had become a self-appointed "mind guard" to the group, threatening outsiders holding opposing opinions and accusing them of disloyalty to the President.
- Where strong groupthink pressures exist, outgroups are ridiculed as "too stupid" to be a threat or "too untrustworthy" to be negotiated with.

The picture . . . therefore, is of a tightly knit group, isolated from outside influences, converging rapidly on to a normatively "correct" point of view and thereafter being convinced of its own rectitude and the inferiority of all other competing opinions (or groups).

(Brown, 2000, p. 213)

Groupthink consists of the following characteristics:

- an illusion of vulnerability,
- excessive optimism and risk taking,
- a tendency to rationalize and discount warnings,
- stereotyping of the opposition,
- self-censorship,
- failure to use expert opinion.

All lead to a failure to solve problems effectively because of a need for unanimity and cohesiveness.

Subsequent research has provided some support for Janis's ideas but by no means all. This suggests that cohesiveness is not an important factor for the emergence of groupthink but that the style of the leader is. Vinokur, Burnstein, Sechrest, and Wortman (1985) studied decision making in six conferences of experts and consumers meeting to evaluate new medical technologies. The results suggested that decision-making processes and outcomes were not affected detrimentally by group cohesiveness, but that processes and outcomes were poorer if the chair of the meetings did not use a facilitative style. The research evidence seems clear that leaders who are very directive inhibit the expression and exploration of opposing opinions, and those who push their own points of view too hard reduce the quality of decision making. If the job is catching wildebeest or diagnosing and treating breast cancer, for examples, the consequences for the team and those they serve can be disastrous. Peterson (1997) added a further piece to the jigsaw of our understanding by showing that leaders who were directive about the ends (trying to achieve their particular goals) inhibited good team decision making. Those who were directive about processes in meetings, encouraging inputs from shyer members and controlling the inputs of the more dominant or unruly members, enabled high quality decision making. What does seem helpful is to discuss how decisions will be made at the start of the discussion, to review the dangers (not discussing unshared information – the hidden profile problem) and to agree to follow some basic ground rules for meetings (see p. 105).

Team Pressures to Conform

The effects of group pressures on individuals to conform are well known. In Asch's research (Asch, 1956) participants were shown into a room to join others already there. Those in the room before the experimental participants were, unbeknown to the experimental participants, confederates of the researcher. A series of vertical lines was flashed on a screen and both participants and "confederates" were asked to determine which of three lines was of the same size as a standard line. These were unambiguous stimuli. On most occasions, the confederates chose the line that equaled the length of the standard line, but on a number of occasions they unanimously picked a wrong line. Fully three-quarters of the experimental participants went along with the majority on at least one occasion, even though subsequently they reported having been aware that this was the incorrect line. They indicated that this was due to a desire not to be different from the majority, especially where the majority was unanimous.

A number of studies have revealed similar effects that majorities have a powerful influence on the behavior of people in teams.

Encouragingly, there are individual differences in the extent to which people will go along with the majority. In Asch's experiments, some individuals (25% of those who participated) never went along with the majority, while others conformed to the majority opinion on all occasions. Moreover, the size of the group is important in influencing the majority influence. The results showed that when an individual was confronted with only one person who was responding in an inconsistent manner, he or she was unlikely to be influenced. Under pressure from a majority of three, conformity jumped to 32 percent, from only 14 percent with a majority of two (Bond & Smith, 1996). If there was another dissenting person in the group, participants answered incorrectly in only 9 percent of cases compared with 36 percent when they were in a minority of one. Moreover, there are cultural differences in the extent to which people will conform (Smith & Bond, 1993); people in collectivist cultures such as China, Japan, and Brazil show a greater tendency to conform to the majority than those in individualistic cultures such as the UK and USA.

 ## Obedience to Authority

In hierarchical groups, there is a tendency for people to be obedient to authority. Within a group situation where there is a dominant leader, people may well be inclined to go along with the leader rather than to assert their own opinions. In a chilling demonstration of this danger, Stanley Milgram examined the extent to which individuals would be obedient to the commands of an experimenter to give electric shocks to an individual learning word pairs (Milgram, 1963, 1965). The person learning the word pairs was in fact a confederate of the experimenter, who faked the electric shocks. Out of 40 people participating in the experiment, 26 obeyed the orders of the experimenter to the end and continued to give (apparent) electric shock punishment to the learners, up to and beyond the point where they were led to believe that the learners had been severely injured. This was despite the fact that in many instances the individuals administering the shocks were clearly suffering great tension and concern about what they were doing. One observer related:

> I observed a mature and initially poised executive enter the laboratory smiling and confident. Within 20 minutes, he was reduced to a twitching,

stuttering wreck that was rapidly approaching a point of nervous collapse. He constantly pulled on his ear lobe, and twisted his hand. At one point, he pushed his fist into his forehead and muttered: "Oh God, let's stop it."

(Milgram, 1963, p. 377)

Yet he continued to listen to every word of the experimenter, and obeyed to the end. This research suggests that there are dangers in team settings that can result in conformity and obedience to authority in the face of clear rational evidence against a given course of action.

◆ Team Defense Mechanisms

If we think of a team as somehow a "living entity" in its own right, it would not be surprising for it to have developed mechanisms to survive in a changing environment. Just like an organism, a team develops an immune system to fight threats to its stability. Often this system is such an integral part of the norms and unwritten rules of the team that it is very difficult to detect. Such team defenses are sometimes referred to as "defensive routines" that are set into motion automatically and without deliberate intention on the part of any individual (Argyris, 1990).

Defensive routines make the unreasonable seem reasonable, and are often employed in the name of caring and diplomacy. One example of a defensive routine is team members continually blaming the organization or another team or department, senior managers, or resources problems, for performance difficulties that the team is experiencing. Therefore, regardless of what goes on within the team, such as a failure to deal with one member not doing their work effectively, team members tend to see problems as caused by circumstances outside the team. Team members maintain a superficial cohesion and collude together in not addressing their performance problems. If the job of the team is to catch wildebeest or to conduct diagnoses of women with breast cancer, the consequences can be disastrous.

At their best, these defensive routines help protect the team from experiencing unnecessary turmoil. They are, however, designed to reduce pain and embarrassment, and in doing so can inhibit team functioning. Moreover, in trying to maintain the status quo, team members may employ defensive routines that prevent the team from dealing with the root causes of problems. The nature of team defensive routines is such that they are often undiscussable, and their undiscussability is also undiscussable!

Exposing defensive routines is all the more difficult because they are so very hard to detect. People become immensely frustrated at the struggle involved in implementing a clearly sensible innovation, particularly when they are unable to understand why it is proving so difficult and why it arouses so much hostility.

Defensive routines are particularly likely to develop in teams within organizations that have "blame cultures." These are places where the reaction to failures, errors, or near misses is to search for someone to blame – someone who can carry all the responsibility for the problem. This is not a learning environment. Instead, team members should encourage learning by asking "*What* not *who* was the underlying cause of the problem and what can we learn from this about how we work?" Also, they can ask "How can we change the way we work so that this problem does not occur again?"

Box 7.1: Overcoming defensive routines

- Have arguments well thought out; reasons should be compelling, vigorous and publicly testable.
- Do not promise more than can be delivered; others can seize on unrealistic promises to reject what is essentially a good idea.
- Encourage team members to discuss mistakes and discourage blaming. Use mistakes as a means of learning (ask "what can we learn from this?").
- Always try to look beneath the surface and encourage team members to do the same. Continually ask "why?" of those who resist the change.
- Surface and bring into the open subjects that seem to be undiscussable, despite the potential hostility this may generate.
- Learn to be aware of when you are involved in or colluding with defensive routines.
- Try to see through the issues of efficiency (doing things right) to the more important questions of effectiveness (doing the right things). Unfortunately, it is probably when team members start asking questions at this level that they meet most resistance.

TEAMWORK IN PRACTICE

◆ A Commitment to Excellence and the Team Task

How can a team function in ways that minimize conformity, obedience to authority, and the effects of defensive routines? They can do this by making outstanding performance of the task their first priority. But structures, strategies, techniques, and norms can also be developed that enable teams to resist these influences effectively. One technique described earlier is the stepladder technique of decision making (see chapter 6). Changing team structure will also reduce hierarchies within the team. Below, we explore also some of the techniques or orientations that can be used for ensuring high quality team performance and decision making (for more methods see West, 1997).

Task focus/constructive controversy

Task focus refers to team members' preparedness to examine their team performance critically. Dean Tjosvold has coined the term "constructive controversy" to describe the conditions necessary for effective questioning within a team (Tjosvold, 1998).

Research evidence amassed by Tjosvold and others suggests that when teams explore opposing opinions carefully and discuss them in a cooperative context, quality of decision making and team effectiveness is dramatically increased (see also West, Tjosvold, & Smith, 2003). "Controversy when discussed in a co-operative context promotes elaboration of views, the search for new information and ideas and the integration of apparently opposing positions" (Tjosvold, 1991, p. 49). Tjosvold believes that a lack of constructive controversy can lead to decisions such as the Bay of Pigs invasion and the Challenger space shuttle disaster. In the latter case, engineers suppressed controversy over the fact that opinions differed about the appropriateness of flying the shuttle in cold weather. Tjosvold argues that there are three elements to controversy: elaborating positions, searching for understanding, and integrating perspectives.

1   First, team members should carefully describe their positions, explaining how they have come to their decisions in relation to any particular issue within the team. They should also indicate to what extent they are confident or uncertain about the positions they have adopted.

2   People with opposing viewpoints should seek out more information about others' positions and attempt to restate them as clearly as possible. There should be attempts to explore areas of common ground in opposing positions, along with an emphasis on personal regard for individuals whose positions oppose their own. This process will lead to greater creativity and outcomes that are more productive.

3   Team members should encourage integration by working to resolve controversy based on the principle of excellence in decision making. Team members should attempt to influence their colleagues toward a solution based on shared rational understanding rather than attempted dominance. Finally, members should strive for consensus by combining team ideas wherever possible rather than using techniques to reduce controversy, such as majority voting. Strategies such as voting may merely postpone controversy. Box 7.2 shows the conditions within which team constructive controversy can exist.

The team's dance will reflect the extent to which all team members engage, contribute, and shape each other's views. All are open to others' reactions to their positions and to having their views shaped or changed by others within the team, regardless of their status in the team. The team is an arena in which all play, strive, and contribute to shaping the team's direction in the interests of their shared vision. In a good sports team, team members talk to each other to encourage better team performance throughout the game.

Devil's advocacy

In order to cope with the potential flaws in his Cabinet's decision-making strategies President Kennedy introduced a number of initiatives. First, he brought alternative and often extreme viewpoints into Cabinet discussions to promote diversity of opinion and more creative decision making. Secondly, he promoted the idea of delaying decisions until they were necessary, rather than rushing to first solutions. Thirdly, he appointed someone within the team to challenge quickly and vigorously any decisions considered by the team. Bobby Kennedy, the then Attorney General, was appointed to this position of devil's advocate. He later described how during the Cuban missile crisis in 1963, his role was to criticize and attack opinions offered within the team in order to ensure that arguments were carefully examined for strengths and weaknesses. This led, he argued, to better quality decision making.

Box 7.2: Encouraging constructive controversy in teams

- Teams can encourage constructive controversy by coaching team members to play with and combine diverse ideas; to explore all team members' views in an open-minded way, so that creative ideas emerge.
- Independent thinking is encouraged by having the team considers all team members' views and suggestions, since this discourages the tendency to conform to the majority view.
- Team members should consider all team members' views based on whether their proposals would improve the team's service to its clients. They base judgements then on quality, not (e.g.) on the status of the person proposing the idea.
- Team members should have vigorous and supportive discussions of alternatives, since such comprehensive decision making encourages all team members to develop their critical thinking and to learn from each other in the course of teamwork.
- As the team practices these creative, rigorous, and open-minded approaches to making decisions and constructively using disagreements, they learn, grow, become more confident in their individual abilities and more skilled in the team dance together.
- Team leaders can encourage team members to explore opposing opinions by having them carefully describe their positions and explain how they have come to their decisions in relation to any particular issue. All team members should also ask them to indicate their confidence or uncertainty about their positions.
- Team members with opposing viewpoints should seek out more information about other team members' positions and attempt to restate them as clearly as possible. Team members can search for ways of integrating opposing positions.
- Leaders should coach team members to strive for consensus by combining team ideas wherever possible rather than using techniques to reduce controversy, such as majority voting (strategies such as voting merely postpone controversy).

Box 7.2: (cont'd)

TEAMWORK IN PRACTICE

- Team leaders can encourage team members not to focus on winning in the process of making decisions. They should be primarily concerned with making excellent decisions that lead to the best products or services for their clients.
- Constructive controversy does not exist when there are competitive team climates. Team members can alert each other if they seem more interested in winning arguments than finding the best solutions.
- Team goals should be primary – shared objectives should steer the work of the team.
- If team members publicly question their colleagues' competence, destructive arguments about team decisions erupt and quality of decision making suffers. Team leaders should discourage such discussions and, if they feel there is a problem of competence, deal with these issues privately.
- Team members should build cooperative team climates, characterized by trust, supportiveness, safety, and a professional approach to work. Leaders can emphasize the team's shared goals because, when team members are aware of their shared goals, they work toward the same end. This unites them and enables them to use disagreement as a means to better quality decision making.
- Leaders should also encourage team members to communicate their respect for each other's competence and commitment. In this way, they will feel that disagreements do not represent attacks on each other's ability and this will be clear to all.

The devil's advocate is the individual within the team whose responsibility it is to challenge arguments and ideas and seek out weaknesses within them. However, research (Nemeth, Rogers, & Brown, 2001) suggests that this is worse than having no devil's advocate. We are impressed and encouraged to think independently only by the courage of genuine dissent in a team. Appointing someone artificially to disagree with the team's view dupes team members into thinking they are genuinely debating issues in a thorough and vigorous way. In fact, such sops to dissent undermine independent thinking and challenging debate. It is the courage of genuine dissent that inspires us to think both more deeply and more independently.

Box 7.3: Constructive controversy

Constructive controversy is necessary for:

- creativity,
- independent thinking,
- quality checking,
- professional development,
- team development.

Constructive controversy involves:

- exploration of opposing opinions,
- open-minded consideration and understanding,
- concern for integration of ideas,
- concern with high quality solutions,
- tolerance of diversity.

Constructive controversy exists when there are:

- cooperative team climates,
- shared team goals,
- personal competence confirmed,
- mutual influence processes.

Constructive controversy does not exist when:

- competitive team climates dominate,
- team goals are not primary,
- team members question each other's personal competence,
- there are processes of attempted dominance.

Negative brainstorming

Negative brainstorming is a particularly useful technique for promoting task focus and critical thinking in teams. It is useful for testing a new proposal, or for evaluating an existing strategy, practice, or objective (West, 1996, 1997). The technique has three steps:

Step 1 Once a promising idea has been proposed (or in the case of an existing practice, the practice or strategy has been clearly identified), the team brainstorms around all possible negative aspects or consequences of the idea. This brainstorming should be as uninhibited as positive brainstorming in the classical approach (see chapter 1). The intention is to generate a list of all the possible negative aspects of the idea or strategy, no matter how wild or fanciful these possibilities might appear.

Step 2 Team members choose four or five of the most salient criticisms, and examine these in more detail. At least one of these criticisms should be a wild or fanciful criticism.

Step 3 The team then considers how the idea or existing practice could be modified to deal with each of the criticisms in turn. This third stage of the process is, therefore, essentially constructive in that the team is seeking to build on a new or existing practice in order to counter the major criticisms of it.

It may be that some fundamental weakness or difficulty is identified, which the team sees no way of overcoming. In this case, the idea or the existing practice may be abandoned. However, this is a benefit rather than a disadvantage of the process since it enables teams to identify at an early stage any idea or approach that is likely to be unsuccessful.

This exercise is useful when an idea has reached the adoption and implementation phase of decision making. In addition to drawing out the weak points of an idea before implementation, it also encourages constructive criticism. People are often afraid of causing offense so they inhibit their criticisms. This approach makes it clear that team members are criticizing ideas and practices rather than people. When it is practiced frequently, team members come to accept "criticizing ideas as a way of improving on them" as good practice.

Stakeholder analysis

This is a useful method for exploring an issue in more depth and improving upon existing and proposed solutions. People are much less resistant to changes as long as the team puts careful and creative thought into considering how those changes will affect them in practice. The technique involves the team acting as if they were each stakeholder group in turn, and considering all the advantages and disadvantages arising from team objectives, strategies, processes, or proposed changes. Stakeholders are all those interested individuals and teams, both internal and external to the team, who affect or who are affected by the team's objectives and practices. Team members then list all possible advantages and disadvantages in relation to the stakeholder group (see the example in Box 7.4). Then team members modify the proposed objective or change in order to minimize the disadvantages to the stakeholder group and/or maximize the advantages. They do this for every major stakeholder in turn.

Box 7.4: Stakeholder analysis in practice

1 Proposed change

A large health care team that has always been run along traditional lines has proposed that it will become an independent practice, more like a self-governing team responsible for its own finances and administration. This proposal constitutes a major shift in team practice and philosophy. Who are the major stakeholders?

2 Identify stakeholders

Patients, patients' relatives and carers, practice nurses, doctors, other staff, the community, professional associations, practice administrators, and managers.

3 Advantages and disadvantages of the change

Patients
Possible advantages: improved speed of service; improved quality of care; improved administration.
Possible disadvantages: the practice has more concern with money than with patients; competition may lead to poorer quality care.

Doctors
Possible advantages: better facilities; quicker decision making; more control over resources.
Possible disadvantages: loss of medical emphasis; administrators will be more concerned with money than with patient care; specialist areas and equipment will be neglected in the interests of satisfying large-scale demand.

Practice Managers
Possible advantages: more power; better quality decision making; clearer managerial responsibilities.
Possible disadvantages: greater accountability; need to generate income; conflict with hospitals or other independent practices.

4 Adapting the change

Having identified potential advantages and disadvantages from the point of view of each stakeholder group, the team then considers how the change can be modified to meet the various concerns, or how the process of change could be managed appropriately to reduce resistance.

TEAMWORK IN PRACTICE

Case study: The manufacturing management team

The Loxley management team consisted of a chief executive, head of production, HR director, R & D director, finance director, sales director, and director of quality. It was a well-established, cohesive, and supportive team. When data from a questionnaire study which they had commissioned was fed back to them they were pleased with the results, but noticed that, in the commentary, their team was described as having few disagreements and little concern with high standards of performance, critical appraisal, and monitoring of colleagues' performance. The team had also voiced anxiety to the facilitator who administered the questionnaire about resistance they were meeting in the hospital when trying to implement changes.

The management team agreed to look at how they managed criticism and disagreement within the team (the climate of excellence) and resistance outside the team. The facilitator working with them urged them also to consider how they shared information and the ways they monitored their decision making and performance. Team members were surprised at the requests since the questionnaire results had generally shown they worked well as a team. It became clear during the feedback meeting that members' commitment to team loyalty and cohesiveness sometimes overrode finding the best solution to problems. This also accounted for the negative reactions from employees that they encountered when implementing management decisions which had not been thought through carefully enough. Team members agreed to ensure they became more visible in the workplace and to use feedback from staff to appraise decisions made within the team. They also agreed to more thoroughly debate issues within the team when they had misgivings rather than agree for the sake of cohesion. Team members went on to use stakeholder analysis to step out of their roles as team members and to think more creatively about problems. The method also enabled the team to think more creatively about problems and to anticipate and therefore reduce resistance from other staff groups.

By carefully considering the effects upon the various stakeholders, team members can make the final objectives or proposed change more resilient. The technique may also alert the team to conflicts they can deal with using appropriate conflict-handling techniques (see chapter 10).

◆ Minority Group Influence in Teams

Many people in large organizations believe that they cannot bring about changes that they see as necessary and valuable. The organization is too big and senior figures oppose the change they wish for. Research on minority group influence suggests otherwise. Minority group influence is the process whereby a minority (in terms of number or power) within a team or society brings about enduring change in the attitudes and behavior of the majority. Exposure to minority group influence appears to cause changes in attitudes in the direction of the "deviant view," but it also produces more creative thinking about issues, as a result of the cognitive or social conflict generated by the minority. Social psychological research on minority influence, therefore, has exciting implications for understanding organizational behaviour.

Traditionally researchers have believed that only majorities in teams and organizations can achieve control, usually through conformity processes. Serge Moscovici and Charlan Nemeth, however, have shown how minorities also influence the thinking and behavior of those with whom they interact (Mosocvici, Mugny, & van Avermaet, 1985; Nemeth & Owens, 1996). Moscovici argues that minority group influence accounts for the influence on public attitudes of the environmental and feminist movements in the 1970s and 1980s. Repeated exposure to a consistent minority view leads to marked and internalized changes in attitudes and behaviors. When people conform to a majority opinion, they generally comply publicly without necessarily changing their private beliefs, as we saw earlier. Minorities, in contrast, appear to produce a shift in private views rather than mere public compliance. Moreover, some evidence suggests that even if they do not cause the majority to adopt their viewpoints, minorities encourage greater creativity in thinking about the specific issues they raise. They cause us to think more comprehensively and critically about the issues (Nemeth, Connell, Rogers, & Brown, 2001).

In one early study of minority influence, participants were shown blue and green slides and asked to categorize them accordingly (Moscovici, Lage, & Naffrechoux, 1969). Those in the experimental group were exposed to a minority of people who consistently categorized some blue slides as green. This procedure had no impact on the majority's correct categorizing of the blue slides. However, when members of the majority were subsequently asked to rate some ambiguous "blue-green" slides, over half identified the slides in a direction consistent with the minority view. A control group that was not exposed to a minority showed no such effects.

Charlan Nemeth suggests that minority influence leads to both creative and independent thinking (Nemeth & Nemeth-Brown, 2003). In one study, researchers exposed participants to a minority of people who consistently judged blue stimuli as green. Subsequently, the same group were placed in a situation where a *majority* incorrectly rated red stimuli as orange. But the experimental group showed almost complete independence and did not differ significantly from control subjects, who made their judgements of the red stimuli alone. Those not exposed to minority dissent first agreed with the majority's incorrect judgement of orange in over 70 percent of trials. Minorities therefore appear to encourage independence of thinking in those around them (see Nemeth & Owens, 1996 for a review).

In a further study of originality, individuals exposed to a minority who consistently rated blue slides as green were asked to respond seven times in a word association exercise to the words "blue" or "green." Those exposed to a minority judgement gave significantly more word associations and with a higher degree of originality than those exposed to a majority view. Nemeth concludes that:

> This work argues for the importance of minority dissent, even dissent that is wrong. Further, we assume that its import lies not in the truth of its position or even in the likelihood that it will prevail. Rather it appears to stimulate divergent thoughts. Issues and problems are considered from more perspectives, and on balance, people detect new solutions and find more correct answers.
>
> **(Nemeth, 1989, p. 9)**

This positive optimistic message suggests that where a minority within the team is powerfully committed to a particular change, by persistence it can achieve greater creativity in team thinking around the issue, albeit at the price of some conflict. In a study of newly formed postal workers' teams in the Netherlands, Carsten De Dreu and I found that minority dissent in teams that were characterized by a high level of participation was associated with high levels of innovation (De Dreu & West, 2001). The exploration of opposing opinions and a concern with excellence are essential elements in team effectiveness, without which teams may flounder in stagnant ponds of mediocrity. With a commitment to excellence in their work, team members can combine their knowledge and skills to create teams that are sparkling fountains of creativity. The next chapter explores these themes by describing the factors that promote creativity and innovation.

Box 7.5: Bringing about change: a minority influence strategy

1   The minority needs a clear and well-developed vision of the purpose and outcome of the change. This should be a single statement. An attractive, appealing, compelling vision statement will, by repetition, encourage the creative thinking of others in the team who were initially opposed to the new proposals.

2   A majority is more likely to accept a minority viewpoint if it is argued coherently and consistently. Therefore, the minority should develop carefully, and repeatedly rehearse the content of the vision as well as the plan for achieving it. Moreover, individuals should ensure that they have at least one ally in the team who will also argue the case. Minorities of two are effective. A minority of one will invariably be ineffective. The greater the degree of unanimity and commitment to the change among the minority members, the more likely is it to be successful.

3   It requires stamina to maintain the change process in the face of frequent setbacks and stiff opposition.

4   In order to manage resistance the minority in the team need to consider carefully all possible objections to the change and build into their arguments ways of responding positively and convincingly. This may mean modifying plans accordingly beforehand (see the discussion on stakeholder analysis above). Team members should develop convincing and well-rehearsed counterarguments. At the same time, it is important to listen actively to other members of the team and to be seen to pay attention to their concerns.

5   Information dissemination is also important in the change process since misunderstanding generates much resistance. The minority in a team should ensure they present coherent and convincing arguments to all other team

TEAMWORK IN PRACTICE

TEAMWORK IN PRACTICE

Box 7.5: (cont'd)

members. They must *prepare, rehearse, present, present, and present again.*

6 If possible the team leader should be committed to and thoroughly rehearsed in the arguments for the change. However, in the absence of support from those hierarchically superior, consistency of argument and repeated presentation is likely to lead to everyone in the team thinking more creatively around the issues over time, though at the price of some conflict in the team.

7 Participation in the change process is the single most effective way of reducing resistance. This may be accomplished by team meetings and sharing of information. It should also be a real attempt to get the views of others in the team about how to accomplish the changes most effectively and what the major obstacles are likely to be.

key revision points:

■ Why is a main focus on task performance in teams important?

■ What are group conformity processes and how do they undermine team performance?

■ What is "groupthink" and under what circumstances is it most likely to arise?

■ What are team defense mechanisms and how can teams overcome them?

■ What is constructive controversy, why is it necessary in teams, and what conditions in teams support it?

■ What techniques can teams use to encourage task focus and excellence in decision making?

■ What is minority group influence in teams and under what conditions will it affect the majority's thinking?

■ How could you use minority influence theory to plan a change strategy for your team?

FURTHER READING

Argyris C. (1990). *Overcoming organizational defenses: Facilitating organizational learning*. Boston, MA: Allyn and Bacon.

Cannon-Bowers, J. A. & Salas, E. (eds.) (1998). *Making decisions under stress: Implications for individual and team training*. Washington, DC: American Psychological Association.

Guzzo, R. A. & Salas, E. (eds.) (1995). *Team effectiveness and decision making in organizations*. San Francisco: Jossey Bass.

Moscovici, S., Mugny, G. & van Avermaet, E. (eds.) (1985). *Perspectives on minority influence*. Cambridge, UK: Cambridge University Press.

Nemeth, C. J. & Nemeth-Brown, B. (2003). Better than individuals? The potential benefits of dissent and diversity for group creativity. In P. Paulus & B. Nijstad (eds.), *Group creativity* (pp. 63–84). Oxford: Oxford University Press.

Nemeth, C., Rogers, J., & Brown, K. (2001). Devil's advocate vs. authentic dissent: Stimulating quantity and quality. *European Journal of Social Psychology, 31*, 707–20.

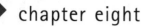

◆ chapter eight

Creative Problem Solving

The most incomprehensible thing about the world is that it is comprehensible.

Albert Einstein

key learning points:

- The difference between team creativity and innovation
- The four climate factors that influence innovation in teams
- The stages of creative problem solving
- Techniques for developing creative ideas in teams

It has become a cliché to speak of rapid change in society. Organizations change with bewildering frequency, as they are privatized, acquired, rationalized, restructured, reorganized, or liquidated. One major cause of this rapid change is the external socio-economic environment within which organizations find themselves. Competition has become a global rather than a national phenomenon. Organizations have become international rather than national. Moreover, the demands of consumers are shifting constantly, as people require new and different commodities and services to meet their needs. Information technology has made our worlds infinitely richer in opportunities and demands.

If we lived in a climate where the weather changed constantly from hour to hour, sometimes hot, sometimes wet, sometimes cold, sometimes snowing, we would have to prepare for every eventuality and adapt quickly. We would have raincoats, cool clothes, umbrellas, warm clothes, and even the occasional shelter as we made our way around. Similarly, in their rapidly changing environment, organizations need to be highly adaptable. Just as human beings have adapted to their environments by finding new and improved ways of organizing societies and work, so organizations too must be innovative in order to survive. They must be innovative.

In response to increasing complexity and change, many organizations have made the team the functional unit of the organization. Instead of individuals being responsible for separate pieces of work, groups of individuals come together to combine their efforts, knowledge, and skills to achieve shared goals. Consequently, for organizations to be innovative, teams also must be innovative, adaptable, and essentially creative in their response to problems both within their organizations and in the wider environment (Henry, 2001; Ford & Gioa, 1995; Runco & Pritzker, 1999a, 1999b). But how?

◆ Team Innovation

Team innovation is the introduction of new and improved ways of doing things by a team. Creativity and innovation are distinguished in the following ways: creativity refers to new ideas, and innovation (which includes creativity) also requires that creative ideas are put into action, within a team, organization, or society. Creativity is the development of ideas; innovation implementation is making them happen in practice. Innovation therefore includes both creativity and implementation (West, 2002).

Figure 8.1 shows a model of team innovation, which emphasizes the importance of some principal factors examined in earlier chapters

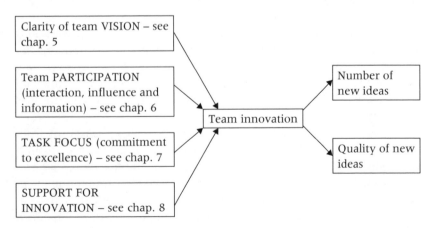

Figure 8.1 A model of team innovation

(West & Anderson, 1996). The model demonstrates how shared vision, task focus (a commitment to excellence), participative safety, and support for innovation all determine the level of a team's innovativeness. In research in a wide variety of organizations, my colleagues and I have shown how these four factors are powerful predictors of team innovation (West, 2002).

Vision/shared objectives

In Chapter 5 we noted that vision partly determines the effectiveness of teams at work. But there is also strong evidence that a clearly stated mission is important in predicting success in innovation. In a major research study of 418 project teams Pinto and Prescott (1987) found that a clearly stated mission predicted success at each stage of the innovation process, that is, conception, planning, execution, and termination.

Participative safety

High levels of participation mean low resistance to change and high levels of innovation in teams. The more people participate in team decision making through having influence, interacting with those involved in change processes, and sharing information, the more likely are they to invest in the outcomes of those decisions and to offer ideas for new and improved ways of working (Amabile, 1997; Heller, Pusić, Strauss, & Wilpert, 1998). The level of safety in the team is also important, since work team members are more likely to take the risk of proposing new ways of working in a climate that they see as nonthreatening and supportive (Edmondson, 1999; Sternberg & Lubart, 1996). There is certainly evidence that among teams of scientists, innovation is high when the atmosphere within the team is warm, supportive, but intellectually demanding (Andrews, 1979; Mumford & Gustafson, 1988).

Task focus or commitment to excellence

In the last chapter, we saw how "groupthink" and "process losses" reduce the effectiveness of team performance and team decision making. Similarly, highly cohesive teams may inhibit attempts at innovation by treating them as deviations from team norms and practices. High levels of participative safety alone might lead to reluctance to challenge

Exercise 8.1: How innovative is your team at work?

Compared with other similar teams how innovative do you consider your team to be. Circle the appropriate response for the following task areas:

	Highly stable: few changes introduced	Moderately innovative: some changes introduced	Highly innovative: many changes introduced
Setting work targets or objectives	1 2	3	4 5
Deciding the methods used to achieve objectives/targets	1 2	3	4 5
Initiating new procedures or information systems	1 2	3	4 5
Developing innovative ways of accomplishing targets/objectives	1 2	3	4 5
Initiating changes in the job contents and work methods of your staff.	1 2	3	4 5

Total score ☐

Administer this questionnaire to all members of your team and calculate the average level of innovation. If the team scores above an average of 4, team members see the team as innovative. Scores of 3 or below should be considered an indication that the team should be more adaptive. This is also dependent upon the context of the team's work. For example, in a hospital, highly innovative surgical teams might not be what is required if standard operating procedures should always be followed. Therefore, when analyzing the questionnaire it is important to bear in mind the context within which the team is working.

poor or even potentially dangerous plans for innovation, on the basis that such challenges would represent a threat to the team's warm interpersonal climate. Indeed, the evidence from research in this area is that minority group influence leads to high levels of conflict but is a major cause of innovation in teams (Nemeth & Owens, 1996). We need to avoid situations in which those who want to introduce innovations in teams see the risk of conflict and so avoid innovation in order to maintain team harmony.

Task focus or commitment to excellence means team members have a shared concern with quality of performance and therefore have systems for evaluation, modification, control, and critical appraisal. Improved task focus will produce innovation by encouraging diversity and creativity, while at the same time ensuring a high quality of innovation via the careful examination of ideas proposed (Tjosvold, 1998).

Support for innovation

Levels of team innovation are high when team members expect, approve, and practically support attempts to introduce new and improved ways of doing things. Team members may reject or ignore ideas or they may offer both verbal and practical support. What is more difficult to recognize is lack of support in teams that are enthusiastic about new ideas but do nothing to help implement them, or whose members passively resist their implementation.

Many teams in organizations, as part of their overall objectives, express support for the development of new and improved ways of working, but they do not provide the practical support to enable the ideas to be put into practice. Some organizational psychologists have shown how organizations have *theories espoused* (the way that they say they work) and *theories in use* (the way that they actually work) (Argyris, 1978).

High levels of both verbal and practical support will lead to more attempts to introduce innovations in teams. Verbal support is most helpful when team members initially propose ideas. Practical support can take the form of cooperation in the development of ideas as well as the provision of time and resources by team members to apply them.

Some teams have difficulty providing even verbal support for innovation. But if people seem inherently resistant to new ideas then teams are likely to propose only those ideas they feel sure about. Minimizing risk by not giving verbal support often means minimizing innovation. A simple technique a team can use to promote support and openness to new ideas in meetings is the "yes, and . . ." method (see Box 8.1).

Box 8.1: The "yes and . . ." method

People often look for faults in a new idea when it is first raised. This can have the effect of reducing enthusiasm and the preparedness of people to offer new ideas. The "yes and . . ." method is a way of avoiding the "no" and "yes, but . . ." traps that are often the end of a new idea. Try saying "yes," and then building on the idea in a meeting before deciding that it will not work. Try to build on the positive or add your own positive idea to the suggestion. This is a simple but very powerful technique, which, if applied as a rule in departmental meetings, can change the climate substantially. It also enables team members to identify quickly the person who finds it hardest not to slip back into "yes, but . . ." ways.

Creative Problem Solving in Teams

We tend to think of problem solving as being a single activity, but a good deal of research indicates that there are a number of distinct and important stages. Each requires different kinds of skills and activities. It is therefore useful to distinguish between the different stages, and to use appropriate skills for each. Four well-established stages are problem exploration, developing alternative ideas, selecting an option, and implementing the preferred option:

Stage 1 – Exploration

↓

Stage 2 – Ideation

↓

Stage 3 – Selection

↓

Stage 4 – Implementation

Stage 1: exploration

Probably the most important stage of team problem solving is clarifying and exploring the problem. Team members usually begin to try to develop solutions to problems before clarifying and exploring and, if necessary, redefining the problem itself. But the more time spent in exploring and clarifying a problem before attempting to seek solutions, the better the quality of the ultimate solution. Moreover, the time saved by careful exploration of problems outweighs the time expended on this task. Problem exploration can take the form of goal focus or stakeholder analysis (see chapter 6).

Stage 2: ideation

Having suspended attempts at solution development during Stage 1, the next step is to develop a range of alternative solutions to the problem as defined. When making decisions, teams generally seek for "one way out." One idea is proposed and the team goes with that idea, making appropriate modifications as are perceived necessary. Research on team problem solving suggests that it is most effective to begin by generating a range of possible solutions. This is the stage when having a safe climate with verbal support for innovation and using "yes, and . . ." responses is particularly important to promote a sense of confidence. Teams can use techniques such as brainstorming (techniques which are described later in this chapter) and it should be a stage that is both playful and challenging, when all ideas are welcomed and encouraged.

Stage 3: selection

Next, the aim is to encourage constructive controversy about appropriate ways forward. It is necessary and desirable to be critical, but this needs to be done in a way that is constructive and personally supportive. If Stage 2 has generated many solutions, it may be necessary to select the three or four solutions that appear most promising, but it is important to avoid selecting only those that fit the current way of doing things. At least one potential solution should be a completely new way of dealing with the issue. In relation to each idea, a stakeholder analysis and/or a negative brainstorming session can be conducted. These techniques enable people to anticipate the likely reactions to proposed solutions. Negative brainstorming also helps to seek out, in a constructive way, all possible defects in the solution suggested, and to remedy these by building on new ideas. Teams should not select a solution simply because it is a solution rather than because it is the *best* solution. In an eagerness to achieve "closure" and avoid further uncertainty or ambiguity, teams are sometimes too prepared to overlook problems inherent in solutions they have adopted.

Stage 4: implementation

Teams that conduct the first three stages carefully will find that implementation is the least difficult and most rewarding stage of the problem-solving process. During this stage teams should be open to possible teething problems that arise and be prepared to modify the implementation process appropriately. At the same time, they should also manage the implementation stage in a way that ensures that the original idea is implemented rather than weakly watered down when the realities of implementation are faced. If we lose the courage of our convictions and go for a compromise it is likely not to satisfy anyone in the team. At the implementation stage, the innovator should gain support in the form of resources, time, and cooperation from others outside the team who may have influence on the effectiveness of the implementation process.

These then are four distinct stages of problem solving. Next we explore techniques that teams can use at each of these stages of creative problem solving (see Van Gundy, 1988; West, 1997).

 ## Techniques for Promoting Creativity Within a Team

Creativity and innovation techniques

These techniques are simply aids and are not themselves magical sources of solutions. Creativity is 95 percent hard work and 5 percent serendipitous discovery. Therefore, when teams use these techniques, members should put in a good deal of effort to see how the ideas they generate can help practically in dealing with the situation the team faces. What will not work is a passive approach that assumes the right answers will just appear as a result of using the techniques.

These creativity techniques provide new and different ways of looking at the issues that teams face, and wild "off the wall" alternatives to existing methods of dealing with challenges.

Technique 1: classical brainstorming

In classical brainstorming, group members produce as many ideas as possible, even utopian or fantastic ideas. The aim is to produce a large quantity of ideas, not necessarily to worry about quality. Judgments are suspended and participants accept all ideas offered. Group members try to use each other's ideas to stimulate more ideas that are new (called "piggy-backing"). So the essential guide-lines are:

- quantity of ideas,
- judgments suspended,
- piggy-backing.

The best way to conduct brainstorming is to give team members an opportunity to generate ideas alone or silently before sharing them with the rest of the team. At this point piggy-backing can occur. The advantage of everyone sharing their ideas is that it produces what is often fruitful social interaction, and confers a sense of participation and involvement in the generation of new ideas for change. It is also valuable to encourage new, wild, different ideas in the brainstorming process, rather than brainstorming simply within the current paradigm of the team. Above all, there should be an element of fun in brainstorming. It is sometimes the wildest craziest ideas that contain within them the seed of a very different and productive new approach to the task or issue that the team is facing.

Technique 2: brainwriting pool

This technique is a variant of classical brainstorming that builds on the superior performance of individuals over groups in brainstorms (see chapter 1) and has the effect of generating very large numbers of ideas within a short space of time. Team members, seated around a table, have blank sheets of paper with space to record ideas. After generating around five to 10 ideas, team members place the sheets in the middle of the table. Each member then continues writing more ideas on the sheets filled in by other team members. They are urged particularly to piggy-back upon the ideas that others have already developed. A session of 20 minutes can produce literally hundreds of ideas from within a team. There is little redundancy because all participants can see the ideas produced by others. Furthermore, team members, while receiving stimulation from the ideas of other members of the team, can proceed at their own pace.

This is a system that teams can use when members of the team find it difficult to get together at the same time. Ideas sheets can be circulated and added to over a period of days. A productive variant of this technique is one made possible by computer networking systems. "Brain-netting" involves setting up a file in a network system to which all team members have access. The problem or issue is headlined at the top of the file and then team members simply add their ideas or suggestions to those of their colleagues within the file. Team members do not need to be together to conduct the brainstorm; moreover, they all have a record of the outcomes of the process.

Technique 3: negative brainstorming

This technique has been described fully in chapter 7 and can be used very effectively to improve creatively on existing or proposed objectives, strategies, work methods, or processes.

Technique 4: goal orientation

The goal orientation technique is useful at the problem exploration and clarification stage and involves critically examining and challenging targets and goals. It can also be used for re-examining the ways in which problems and ideas are defined. This is invaluable in encouraging team members to identify and challenge basic assumptions that are often taken for granted. The approach leads to the framing of new targets and goals, and there are usually many more than were originally identified by the team. The formula of preceding goals with the words "how to . . ." or "I wish . . ." is helpful for clarifying goals. Try to list as many "how to . . ." and "I wish . . ." goals as possible. Then the team should decide which are the most desirable, important, necessary, creative, visionary, practical, attainable, and so on, and begin to develop practical action plans to try to achieve them.

Example: How to deal with traffic jams:

How to reduce the number of cars on the road.
How to get bigger roads.
I wish we could get rid of traffic altogether.
How to get instant teleporting.
How to stop travel.
I wish we could shrink cars.
How to control traffic flow.
How to get lots of people in each vehicle.
I wish we could coordinate travelling plans.
How to always go by plane.
I wish I could hitchhike everywhere.

Technique 5: table of elements

The table of elements is a technique for breaking a problem or issue down into a set of elements or components, brainstorming within each, and then choosing from among the various components those ideas that seem most promising or creative in taking the team forward. It generates an enormous number of potential solutions to a problem in a very short space of time. It is only suitable for problems or issues that can be broken down into components and elements.

Example: A social event

The team has to come up with an idea for a novel social event that will bring people together for a good time outside work. The elements of this problem could be identified as the people who will come to the event; where the event will be held; what activities will take place; when the event will be held; what the purpose of the event will be. The team then brainstorms ideas under each of these elements, or headings (see Table 8.1). The next stage involves choosing potentially wild or promising ideas from among the many combinations of possibilities generated by the table of elements. In this exercise, it is worth throwing in quite different ideas within each part of the brainstorm in order to enable team members to break out of existing ways of thinking. Participants can also choose an array of items from within the elements purely at random (i.e., stick a pin in each column to produce a novel combination). Inevitably, such strategies generate solutions that may appear outlandish or nonsensical at first sight. The purpose of these exercises is, however, to stimulate new ways of looking at problems and this provides 5 percent of the creativity. The other 95 percent comes from the team in seeking to make the wild idea into a workable option. For example, if the following items are selected

- children only
- Bahamas
- treasure hunt
- weekend
- learning to swim

it is possible to combine them into the following more practical solution:

At the weekend social event at a swimming pool, an activity especially designed for the children of team members could be arranged (children only). It could involve a game of pirates (learning to swim), looking for gold tokens (treasure hunt) on a treasure island (Bahamas).

The process of using the table of elements takes only 10 or 15 minutes to complete, but can generate literally tens of thousands of ideas within that time.

Table 8.1 Table of elements: A novel social event

People	Place	Activities	Time	Purpose
Team members	Restaurant	Raise money for charity	Weekend	Learning to swim
Team members and partners	Park	Get to know each other	Friday evening	
Children only	Boat	Have a good time		
Team members and customers	Paris	As a reward		
Handicapped children	Bahamas	Treasure hunt		
Partners only	Motorway	Learn new language		
Team members' pets	Beach	Play golf		
	Swimming pool	Play tennis		
	Hotel			
	Theater			

Technique 6: stakeholder analysis

This is described in chapter 7 and is a way of thinking through change proposals or team objectives from the perspectives of those principally affected by the team's work. It can provide valuable direction for teams in modifying change proposals or objectives appropriately.

 Using Creativity Techniques in Team Meetings

It takes courage to use these creativity techniques in team meetings. As with any new idea, some team members may respond with only half-hearted support, others with ridicule, and still others with outright resistance. All creativity and innovation involves taking risks and, if the team is persistent and confident in introducing the techniques, they will work. It is rather like jumping off a high diving board: you have to have a go at it and take the plunge. In teams, you have to keep trying in order to develop skill and confidence in using new techniques.

It is helpful also to string together a number of these creative techniques. How this is done is itself an opportunity to be creative. Remember the importance of the four steps of problem solving mentioned above when putting a team session together: exploration, ideation, selection, and implementation.

Think carefully about how to use time in team meetings, and which creativity techniques to try. You should allocate sufficient time for each technique so that the team is neither too rushed nor too bored during their application. Make sure the team has a facilitator who understands the use of the techniques and does the job of a facilitator rather than dictates or controls. There should also be sufficient materials for recording ideas, such as flip charts and whiteboards.

In recording people's ideas in a team, the facilitator should write exactly what the individual has said (whenever possible). It is appropriate occasionally to paraphrase a particularly long contribution, but only with the agreement of the individual who has made the proposal. Check the wording with them and see that they are happy with what you have produced. Try to note every contribution, especially those that are humorous or throwaway comments, since they can be a good source of creative ideas. To help create the right sort of climate in a team for creativity, agree some ground rules before getting started. You can write these on a flip chart to act as a reminder throughout the session.

Ground rules will vary according to the particular aims of the team. A typical set of ground rules for a creative session might well include:

- be concise,
- show interest and support,
- jot down all stray thoughts,
- suspend judgment,
- say "yes and . . ." rather than "yes but . . . ,"
- take risks – include the unusual and strange.

If the flow of ideas is drying up, try taking a creative break from the problem. There are numerous ways of doing this, such as word association games, going out for walks, story telling.

◆ Other Influences on Team Innovation

Teams do not exist in isolation, and multiple factors determine the creativity and innovativeness of teams. Extensive research indicates that the climate of the team – vision, participative safety, task focus, and support for innovation – principally determines the level of team innovation (West, 2002). But other factors are also important. Box 8.2 describes how, taking account of relevant research into these other influences, you can facilitate creativity and innovation in your team.

This chapter has examined ways in which teams can promote innovation and creativity in order to remain adaptable and effective within their organizations. In one study of over 2,000 male and female British managers, we found that the vast majority had introduced new and improved ways of doing things when they changed jobs (Nicholson & West, 1988). They changed the objectives of their jobs, the methods, scheduling, practices, and procedures and even the people they dealt with and how they dealt with them. It is significant that in the job changing process, people moving into existing jobs are highly innovative – molding and improving the jobs to fit their way of doing things. Moreover, people who have the opportunity to be innovative at work, introducing new and improved ways of doing things, are far more satisfied with their jobs than those who do not have such opportunities. It was a remarkable finding in the study that, among those who took a job move leading to reduced opportunities for innovation, the negative effects upon their mental health were greater even than among those managers and professionals who had become unemployed.

Box 8.2: Fostering team creativity and innovation

There are a number of simple steps you can take to encourage creativity and innovation in your team. The first is to *decide together to be a creative team.* The decision to be creative and support creativity in the team is a major step. Then *recognize that creativity and innovation are not easy* and encourage team members to be aware of this. People resist change very often in organizations, so conflict is a common characteristic of innovation. Questioning the person who comes up with an idea too closely, joking about the proposal (even in a light way), or simply ignoring the proposal may well lead to the person feeling defensive, which tends to reduce their creativity and that of everyone else in the group. To ensure your team is creative *select diverse people with diverse experience and knowledge.* Innovation requires diversity of knowledge bases, professional orientations, and disciplinary backgrounds. These diverse perspectives can lead to radical innovations. This also requires a high level of integration. The members of your team have to be clear about and committed to their shared objectives. And they need to participate in decision making effectively.

It is important that you *build a supportive team.* We think creatively when we feel free from pressure, and when we feel safe and positive. Experimental manipulations of stress levels have shown that higher levels of stress lead to greater reliance on our usual solutions and much less creative thinking (Claxton, 1998a, 1998b). When we feel positive emotions we are both more creative and more cooperative. So create a positive emotional environment. Paradoxically, you must also *challenge the team – hard!* Teams innovate most (i.e., they implement their creative ideas in practice) when they are under pressure (West, 2002). The assertion that "necessity is the mother of invention" is based on sound understanding of human behavior. So make sure the team task is truly challenging and stretching and constantly encourage team members to feel the team can accomplish the task. Emphasize the importance of creativity and innovation and not just productivity or other performance measures. That way people will learn that you really do value creativity. But also *make team members stop work* in order to be creative. Your team needs to stop work from time to time (at least every six months) in order to remind themselves or discover what it is they are really trying to achieve, and to review the ways the team is going about the task. Then they can reaffirm or change direction, improve ways of working, and generate more ideas for new and improved services for clients.

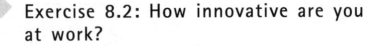

Exercise 8.2: How innovative are you at work?

The following questionnaire explores your feelings about innovation and change at work. How far do you agree or disagree with the following statements (indicate the appropriate number)?

	Strongly disagree	Disagree	Not sure	Agree	Strongly agree
	1	2	3	4	5
I try to introduce improved methods of doing things at work.	[ ]	[ ]	[ ]	[ ]	[ ]
I have ideas which significantly improve the way the job is done.	[ ]	[ ]	[ ]	[ ]	[ ]
I suggest new working methods to the people I work with.	[ ]	[ ]	[ ]	[ ]	[ ]
I contribute to changes in the way my team works.	[ ]	[ ]	[ ]	[ ]	[ ]
I am receptive to new ideas that I can use to improve things at work.	[ ]	[ ]	[ ]	[ ]	[ ]

The average score for 250 employed males and females on this scale was 19.0. If you score 20 or over you have a high propensity to innovate. Take the average score for your team to determine whether your team has a high or low propensity to innovate. If the average score is high, it is more likely the team will produce creative ideas.

The opportunity to be creative and innovative at work is central to our well-being (Marmot, Siegrist, Theorell, & Feeney, 1999). Having our need to be creative and innovative met is a major source of satisfaction for us at work. Teams have an overwhelming influence on the extent to which people are able to be creative in their workplace; a team climate supportive of innovation is crucial (Oldham & Cummings, 1996). It is through attention to creating a climate in which people are clear about their objectives, have a sense of safety with their fellow team members, experience high levels of participation, and emphasize excellence in the work that the individual desire to innovate is translated into practical team outcomes, which promote both team effectiveness and team member well-being.

key revision points:

■ What are creativity and innovation?

■ What four climate factors most influence team innovation?

■ What are the four stages of creative problem solving and which should demand most attention?

■ What techniques can a team use to develop creative ideas?

■ How could you use these in practice in a team meeting?

■ What should a team leader do to encourage team creativity and innovation?

FURTHER READING

Amabile, T. M. (1997). Motivating creativity in organizations: On doing what you love and loving what you do. *California Management Review, 40*, 39–58.

C. M. Ford & Gioia, D. A. (eds.) (1995). *Creative action in organizations: Ivory tower visions and real world voices*. London: Sage Publications.

Claxton, G. (1998). *Hare brain tortoise mind – why intelligence increases when you think less*. London: Fourth Estate Ltd.

Ford, C. M. & Gioia, D. A. (1995). *Creative action in organisations*. London: Sage.

Runco, M. A. & Pritzker, S. R. (1999a). *Encyclopaedia of creativity, vol. 1, A-H*. London: Academic Press.

Runco, M. A. & Pritzker, S. R. (1999b). *Encyclopaedia of creativity*, vol. 2, I-Z. London: Academic Press.

Van Gundy, Jr, A. B. (1988). *Techniques of structured problem solving*. New York: Van Nostrand Reinhold.

West, M. A. & Farr, J. L. (1990). *Innovation and creativity at work: Psychological and organizational strategies*. Chichester, UK: John Wiley & Sons.

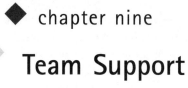

◆ chapter nine

Team Support

False friendship, like the ivy, decays and ruins the walls it embraces; but true friendship gives new life and animation to the object it supports.

Richard Burton

---

key learning points:

■ The importance of emotions in understanding teams

■ The four social dimensions of team working

■ The four types of social support and how they affect team members

■ How teams can support members' growth and development

■ How to build a positive social climate

The fundamental human drive and pervasive motivation to form and maintain lasting, positive, and significant relationships helps us to understand the functioning of teams at work, and in particular the emotions manifested in work groups. Satisfying this need to belong, according to Baumeister and Leary (1995), requires that all our relationships (including those in work teams) are characterized by:

• frequent interaction,
• sense of stability and continuity,
• mutual support and concern,
• freedom from chronic conflict.

Most current research and theories about the functioning of teams fail to take account of the solid evolutionary basis of our tendency to form strong attachments, and by extension to live and work in groups. Human beings work and live in groups because groups enable survival and reproduction. By living and working in groups early humans could share food, easily find mates, and care for infants. They could hunt more effectively and defend themselves against their enemies. Individuals who did not readily join groups would be disadvantaged in comparison with group members as a consequence. The need to belong, which is at the root of our tendency to live and work in groups, is manifested most profoundly in the behavior of children and infants. Children who stuck close to adults were more likely to survive and to be able to reproduce, because they would be protected from danger, cared for, and provided with food. And we see across all societies that when there is danger, illness, or the darkness of nights people have a desire to be with others, indicating the protection offered by group membership. Adults who formed attachments would be more likely to reproduce, and adults who formed long-term relationships would stand a greater chance of producing infants who would grow to reproductive age. "Over the course of evolution, the small group became the basic survival strategy developed by the human species" (Barchas, 1986, p. 212).

This fundamental human motivation to belong therefore shapes much human behavior and for our purposes helps to explain emotional reactions in teams. The absence of one or more of the characteristics of belongingness (frequent interaction, likely continuity and stability, mutual support and concern, and freedom from chronic conflict and negative feeling) will lead to conflict and disintegration within relationships and teams. Our tendency to concentrate on task characteristics and organizational contexts often blinds us to these fundamental socioemotional requirements of team-based working. For the benefits of team working are both improved task performance (West, 1997) and emotional well-being for team members (Carter & West, 1999).

By recognizing the influence of the need to belong upon the behavior of individuals in teams we can come to understand something of the range and underlying causes of emotions in teams. Being accepted, included, and welcomed in the team will lead to feelings of happiness, elation, contentment, and calm. Being rejected, excluded, or ignored will lead to feelings of anxiety, depression, grief, jealousy, or loneliness. Team members' emotional reactions will be stimulated by real, potential, or imagined changes in their belongingness within their work team. Real, potential, or imagined increases in belongingness will lead to an increase in positive individual and team-level affect. Decreases in belongingness will be associated with threats to the individual and a sense of deprivation that will lead to negative affect. Below we consider the effects of the need to belong upon positive and negative emotions and attitudes.

Teams play important roles in enabling people to cope with everyday work challenges and in providing the social and emotional support that contribute to the quality of our lives, both at work and more generally. In our research, we have found that people working in teams are less stressed than those working alone, or in looser groupings (e.g., departments) (Carter & West, 1999). There are important differences too in the job-related mental health of those who undertake demanding and monotonous tasks between those who do and do not have opportunities for social contact with work colleagues through the day. Those who can chat to and joke with other workers suffer fewer problems of job-related mental health than those who, because of noise or the design of their jobs, are unable to enjoy conversation with those around them (Cohen & Wills, 1985; Ganster, Fusilier, & Mayes, 1986; Manning, Jackson, & Fusilier, 1996). Team support is therefore an important element in conceptions of team effectiveness. Moreover, the better the functioning of the team (in relation to the four climate factors) we described in the previous chapter, the less stressed are team members.

 ## The Emotional Life of Teams

When a new work team is formed, team members experience positive emotions and it is a cause for celebration. When new members join teams too there is much positive emotion and many warm expressions of welcome. Team members can encourage this by ensuring there are rituals to welcome new members. Encouraging two-way relationships in the teams is helpful since satisfaction in relationships is a consequence of both the costs as well as the rewards of team membership. One-way relationships in which we only give or only receive are uncomfortable for us, so we are happier in teams in which all members both give and receive support (Baumeister, Wotman, & Stillwell, 1993).

What about negative emotions? Our basic anxiety results from a feeling of being isolated and helpless in a potentially hostile world. Not surprisingly then, we get anxious at the prospect of losing our relationships or at threats of social exclusion. Frequent member changes and threatened dissolution of the team cause anxiety. High levels of conflict too produce anxiety since team members are likely to develop a tense watchfulness in anticipation of conflict. Team leaders can minimize anxiety by ensuring stability of team membership and resolving conflicts early. If the team has to disband, they can prepare team members in advance and mark the ending with a celebration of the team's success.

Team members feel jealous when they feel excluded by, or are less in the favor of, a particularly powerful or attractive team member – especially if it is the team manager. Team leaders should give attention and support to all team members and not just those they feel personally compatible with or who they feel are most competent. Loneliness, in contrast, is not simply a result of lack of contact with others. There are no differences in levels of social contact between those who are lonely and those who are not (Williams & Solano, 1983). The crucial factor is spending time with the people you are close to. Team members who work in multiple teams or short-lived project teams will have many social contacts, but may feel lonely because they cannot develop close ties. They should be encouraged to have a "home team" where they spend more time, get more social support, and discuss their learning needs.

We experience grief at the loss of relationships. When couples divorce, even where they mutually agree on the desirability of the end of their relationships, they typically experience grief. In teams, the departure of members also causes grief. The departing individuals are particularly likely to feel grief, since they lose a whole team. Celebrations of the individual's contribution at a leaving party can help all, and particularly the departing member, to cope with the loss.

Team members can best manage emotions in teams by providing each other with strong social and emotional support. Below we examine the three principal social dimensions of team working: social support, support for growth and development and social climate. Each of these dimensions contributes to team member well-being and long-term team viability, as indicated in Figure 9.1.

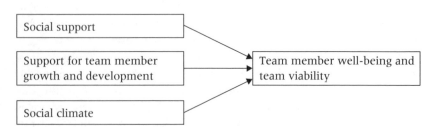

Figure 9.1 The social dimensions of team working

Social Support

There are four main types of social support: emotional, instrumental, informational, and appraisal, and one then needs to distinguish between verbal and enacted support.

Emotional support

This is the kind of social support that we most readily identify. It is the notion of a shoulder to cry on, an encouraging word and sympathetic understanding of another's emotional pain:

Case example

Louise, a nurse, had been visiting one particular family on an intensive basis. The family had a baby, Jonathan, who was at some risk of sudden infant death syndrome (SIDS). On Tuesday morning, Louise arrived in her office to discover that baby Jonathan had been rushed to the hospital in the early hours of the morning, only to be pronounced dead on arrival. The child had all the classic signs of SIDS.

Louise was shocked and upset and immediately called her manager to inform her of the tragic event. Her manager listened briefly to what Louise had to say, then carefully informed her of the steps that she must take to inform the local Health Authority and advised her of the importance of writing up her notes very quickly. The manager told Louise that they would get a chance to talk again in a couple of weeks when she next visited Louise's locality. Louise put down the phone and felt a mixture of grief and frustration. Her grief and emotional burdens were unchanged. On the contrary, they were heavier and complicated by a frustration with her manager demanding immediate bureaucratic action in response to the event.

One of Louise's colleagues then arrived in the office and, knowing how frequently Louise had been visiting Jonathan and his family, said she sympathized, acknowledging how terribly upset Louise must feel about the event. Louise then began to cry and her colleague put an arm around her in comfort.

Later in the day they met to talk again and the colleague, by listening and being supportive, enabled Louise to talk about her own feelings of guilt that she had not done enough to prevent the death. Louise felt guilty at not being more assertive in insisting that the baby was admitted for observation and nutritional support. By expressing the guilt and discussing the feelings with her colleague over the ensuing weeks, Louise was able to work through these feelings and cope.

Here is an example of a colleague providing emotional support both immediately when the support was most urgently needed, and on a continuing basis. Emotional support involves being an active open listener. It does not involve giving advice or direction, rather it is simply providing the space within which people can express their emotions. It also involves a sense of caring toward the person receiving the support. Louise's colleague understood the grief she must feel and enabled her to express that by acknowledging it openly, placing her arms around her and giving her permission to cry. Finally, the colleague offered the opportunity for continued emotional support rather than withdrawing too swiftly.

To what extent should team members provide emotional support for nonwork-related difficulties such as marital difficulties, death in the family, illness, or financial problems? If a colleague is experiencing emotional difficulties related to their lives outside work, it is often desirable and necessary that team colleagues should provide support. But a line has to be drawn between team members offering appropriate and valuable emotional support to colleagues and delving inappropriately into one another's private lives without invitation in ways that might undermine work relationships. There is no simple rule since it depends very much on relationships between team members and the particular circumstances in which people find themselves. Involvement in a team member's personal life should only happen where there is a clear invitation or request from that team member. Sometimes colleagues at work can appear somewhat predatory in their desire to involve themselves in the emotional lives of those around them. This can be destructive for individuals as well as potentially damaging to working relationships. Remember, the primary purpose of the team at work is to complete a task, do a job, achieve its objectives. When building relationships becomes the primary focus, the team is likely to fail its clients and customers, and may well end in interpersonal conflict.

There are some emotional difficulties that require professional help. Where a team member is frequently or deeply depressed, where problems of drug abuse or alcoholism are evident, or where an individual appears suicidal, team members should recommend to such colleagues that they seek professional advice and help. It is important that team members know the limitations of their competence in providing emotional support rather than attempting to provide professional counseling. Many organizations now employ the services of a counselor or a counseling agency, however, and these should usually be a first rather than a last resort.

Informational support

Social support is not only about being warm, empathic, and caring. It is also about doing practical things to aid team members:

Case example:

Sarah, the nurse in a health care team, is responsible for regularly checking up on David, a 12-year-old anorexic boy. But as she was becoming increasingly anxious about David's weight loss and depression, she went to speak with Kate, one of the doctors. Kate was sympathetic and listened attentively to Sarah's anxieties. At the same time, she advised Sarah to contact the Atkinson Morley Hospital in London, which specializes in the treatment of eating disorders. Kate suggested that Sarah talk with the head of the relevant department at the hospital to see whether the child should be admitted. Sarah was able to use Kate's information about the name of the hospital, the specialist, and their telephone number in order to make contact and get expert advice. As a consequence, Sarah's anxiety was somewhat relieved and she was given practical means for aiding David in his illness.

In this case, informational social support has valuable consequences. The extent to which team members provide each other with

informational support of this kind is an important element in the overall social supportiveness of the team.

Instrumental support

Instrumental support refers to the practical, "doing," support that team members offer to one another.

Case examples:

- Jenny, a teacher, had received a call from her childminder to say that her daughter was unwell. She wanted to go home quickly, but had another lesson before the end of school, which she was reluctant to cancel because of important work that the children were due to do. Her colleague, overhearing the conversation, offered to get permission to take the final class for her, enabling Jenny to go home.

- A receptionist in an advertising agency was overloaded with paperwork as she tried to put together the notes of clients due to see the advertising executives that morning. Her colleague, seeing her overloaded, took half of the pile in order to relieve her of some of the work.

- A researcher needed to find an organization within which she could try out a questionnaire she was developing which looked at team effectiveness in organizations. Her colleague telephoned three or four different people he knew in different organizations who he thought might be willing to provide access for her to conduct her questionnaire study. He negotiated with each and, finding one who was willing, then provided the name and address to the researcher.

These are all examples of instrumental support where one team member provides practical action to aid another in achieving the goals that they were aiming for. This may occur in a situation of crisis or simply as part of routine work. Social support in whatever form and at whatever time has an important impact upon the social climate, the well-being of team members, and the viability of a team.

Appraisal support

Team members can provide useful social support by helping their colleagues in the process of making sense of or interpreting a problem situation. This need not involve offering solutions, but would involve helping the individual examine a range of alternative appraisals of any given problem situations.

Case example:

Many individuals face job insecurity and Chris was one of them. He had worked in the same organization for 15 years but suddenly found that the future of the organization was in jeopardy, as its performance had not matched expectations. He then talked with two of his team colleagues about his own future as they discussed possible options. They suggested that there were two or three career possibilities within the parent organization for him, but also that there may be other better opportunities outside. They offered appraisals of the situation which ranged from the most threatening – unemployment – through to seeing the situation as one that was full of potential and promise for Chris (since it might give him the opportunity to specialize in areas that previously had been denied him because of the demands of the organization). Chris began to see that there were important positive opportunities in the situation and that it was not as threatening as he had first thought. He decided to explore with much more vigor the various alternatives open to him and succeeded in landing a job that offered more opportunities for growth and development than the one he had previously occupied.

Here is an example of an individual whose colleagues provided appraisal support that enabled him to deal with his predicament in a constructive and positive way. The way colleagues within teams help us to appraise situations can therefore be an important contributor to the overall social climate of the team.

The more that team members support each other, the more cohesive the team becomes. This leads to better mental health of team members since we know there is a strong and positive relationship between social support at work and job-related mental health (Ganster et al., 1986; Manning et al., 1996).

◆ Support for Team Member Growth and Development

Opportunities for learning, growth, and development are of enormous importance to people's job satisfaction. Those who find themselves in mundane, monotonous, repetitive jobs are usually much less happy at work than those whose jobs are challenging and provide opportunities for new learning and development (Hackman & Oldham, 1976). The latter tend to be more committed to their jobs, their teams, and their organizations and are consequently more productive.

The process of growth and development planning enables people to assess themselves realistically, and then determine their skill, training, and development needs. Team members can work together in planning ways of meeting their needs for growth and development and in providing feedback about skills and strengths. Such team-based growth and development planning also improves communication and understanding between team members, leading to shared understanding about needs, goals, values, and strengths.

Skill development

One way of beginning this process is for team members to list their own and others' strengths, skills, and principal weaknesses. This enables the team both to ask and to answer important questions: what skills would team members like to develop further? Do team members have the opportunity to develop these skills in their current jobs? What professional or technical skills do team members want to develop further? How can the team get the training or support to enable its members to develop these skills? What support can the team offer to ensure individual team members get the training and development opportunities they want?

Job enrichment

It is useful for the team to consider how team members' roles can be enriched or enlarged to make them more fulfilling and satisfying (Hackman & Oldham, 1976). In particular, how could jobs within the team be changed to enable team members to achieve more of their goals; to align their jobs more appropriately with their values, interests, and skills; and to provide opportunities for development, challenge, and change? The characteristics of work roles influence team member learning and well-being, and their creativity and innovation (Hackman & Oldham, 1976; Oldham & Cummings, 1996). There are five core *job characteristics* that can be enriched: skill variety, task identity, task significance, autonomy, and task feedback.

Skill variety refers to the degree to which a job requires different activities in order for the work to be carried out, and the degree to which the range of skills and talents of the person working within the role is used. Thus a nurse working with elderly people in their homes may need to use her professional skills of dressing wounds, listening, counseling, being empathic, and appraising the supports and dangers in the person's home. *Task identity* is the degree to which the job represents a whole piece of work. It is not simply adding a rubber band to the packaging of a product, but being involved in the manufacture of the product throughout the process, or at least in a meaningful part of the process. *Significance* of the task in terms of its impact upon other people within the organization, or in the world at large, has an influence on creativity. Monitoring the effectiveness of an organization's debt collection is less significant than addressing the well-being of elderly people in rural settings, and may therefore evoke less creativity. *Autonomy* refers to the freedom, independence, and discretion for the people performing tasks, in determining how to do their work and when to do it. When people receive *feedback* on their performance they are more likely to become aware of the "performance gaps." Consequently they are more attuned to the need to initiate new ways of working in order to fill the gaps. Of course this also implies they have clear job objectives. Team members can discuss how their roles could be enriched on each of these core job dimensions.

Exercise 9.1: A team exercise to promote job enrichment

Enrich jobs by asking team members to help each other find answers to the following questions (the answers below are in the context of a health care team):

What would you add to or take out from your work objectives in order to enrich or enlarge your job?
I would add the chance to liaise directly with patients over their problems and requirements from the practice. The current method of feedback

Exercise 9.1: (*cont'd*)

through comments sheets placed in the reception area creates too much
formality and is an obstacle to direct communication.

How would you change the methods that you use to achieve
work objectives in order to enrich the job?
There would be much more communication within the team about the
health of whole families, rather than just individuals within families in
relation to treatment and care.

How would you change the scheduling of the work that you do,
i.e. the order in which different parts of the job are done in
order to make the job more satisfying to you?
I would deal with medical records for just one hour in the morning and
then write reports and do telephoning after that. I'd keep the afternoons
free for meetings with other members of the team rather than do all
these things jumbled up.

Which individuals, teams, or organizations would you work with
more (or less) in order to enrich the job and make it more
satisfying for you?
I would work more directly with the GPs and the counselor in considering
the needs of particular families or patients.

In what ways would you liaise differently with the people with
whom you work to make the job more satisfying for you?
I would like team members to take more initiative and share responsib-
ility for team objectives so that I have less of a directive role as a GP.

In what areas of the job would you like the freedom and resources to introduce new and improved ways of doing things?
I'd like to work in a smaller subteam within the practice working solely
on identifying new and improved ways of providing services for clients.

Working with other team members to examine these issues
from your particular standpoint makes job enrichment more
possible than doing the exercise in isolation. Team members
can then play a socially supportive role in helping the individual
find the time to get additional training in order to facilitate job
enrichment.

◆ Balance Between Home and Work Life

One of the mistakes we make is to separate our work lives off from the rest of our lives and to treat work as though it were somehow the only important part of life. We all have to find ways of integrating the demands of work life with the demands and needs that we have in our nonwork lives. An intrinsic part of growth and development planning is considering our personal goals and finding ways of integrating our work-related goals with them. The team can help in enabling or supporting the individual in finding a balance between home and work life. Indeed, those who do achieve such a balance are likely to bring the richness of their nonwork lives to the team and to their work. Those who fail to find a balance are less likely to work effectively within the team (Shore & Barksdale, 1998; Wlliams & Alliger, 1994; Frone, 2000).

Case example:

Debbie was a new lecturer in a university who had lived apart from her partner while they both undertook training. In her new role, it seemed clear that she would again be unable to see much of her partner while he finished his training in another city. Her team discussed how they could help. They agreed that she should do all her lecturing in the first two of the three terms so that she could spend more time in the third term writing chapters and books based on her research, and living with her partner. They also agreed that she should share the courses she taught with another team member so that she could have five-day weekends every other week in order to spend time with her partner. This creative way of managing the team's work enabled Debbie to spend much more time than she had planned with her partner. It was a temporary arrangement for two years until her partner finished his training but it was hugely important to her. She felt immensely committed to the team as a consequence, was highly productive in her research because she had substantial blocks of time for writing, and made an extra effort with her teaching to ensure it was an outstanding success in the unusual circumstances. Finding creative ways of helping team members to keep a good work and home life balance is seen as part of their responsibility by members of well-functioning teams.

◆ Social Climate

The general social climate of a team is a product both of team task processes described in previous chapters as well as the social processes described earlier in this chapter. There are some additional simple rules of intrateam conduct that can help the quality of overall relationships within the team such as the politeness of team members taking the time to greet each other in the morning, or enquiring after the success of nonwork events in colleagues' lives such as birthdays, weddings, and holidays. Taking the time to show interest and concern about the lives of others in the team is a simple and symbolic way of affirming relationships and caring – a kind of "social grooming." Other symbols of warmth and regard, commonly used in teams, are giving of birthday cards and celebrating the successes of individual team members. I have seen the corrosive effects on team social climate of the failure of managers to observe basic rules of politeness and to nurture warmth in the team by (among other sorry examples) not saying "good morning" to junior staff as they arrive for work each morning. Warm, positive, enthusiastic optimism encourages a sense of belonging and community within the workplace.

Another positive element in team social climate is *humor*. Nonaggressive humor is a rich source of positive feeling within the team, encouraging both closer team relationships and creativity. By developing a relaxed enjoyable atmosphere, team members are likely to be committed to the team and to enjoy their jobs. Humor is also a form of creative play that fosters an ethos of innovation within a team (Barsade & Gibson, 1998). Research on humor at work reveals that jokes can stimulate creativity and encourage the development of trust in teams (Clouse & Spurgeon, 1995). Moreover, successful leaders tend to use humor many times more often than others (Goleman, Boyatzis, & McKee, 2002).

More formal approaches to promoting a positive team climate are also useful, such as parties at team members' homes, shared activities such as fitness routines, jogging, football games (which involve both genders), and other sporting activities such as badminton and swimming. In my current team, we sometimes get together at a social function or to attend a theater production or jazz concert. At Christmas the team tends to go out together for a shared lunch. These events are clearly optional and are attended less by team members who have young families than those without. The ongoing nonwork-related interactions promote relationships in the team that contribute to the overall social climate.

◆ Conclusions

The message of this chapter is that the three social dimensions of team functioning (social support, support for growth and development, and general social climate) influence the team's longer term viability, but also impact upon the mental health and job satisfaction of individual team members. In short, teams are communities and we should nurture them. Psychologists may sometimes overcomplicate what are relatively simple aspects of human behavior, and perhaps the most unguarded message of this chapter is that team members can help each other and themselves by caring for one another in the work setting. The message of all the major world religions is the same: that our purpose in any sphere of activity should be to care for those around us. The Dalai Lama expresses this simple principle in his repeated clear prescription: "be kind to one another." This should apply no less in the world of work.

key revision points:

- Why are emotions in teams important to consider?

- What are the four dimensions of belonging?

- What are the four forms of social support in teams?

- What are the three elements involved in supporting the growth and development of team members?

- How can teams build a positive social climate?

FURTHER READING

Baumeister, R. F. & Leary, M. R. (1995). The need to belong: Desire for interpersonal attachments as a fundamental human motivation. *Psychological Bulletin, 117*, 497–529.

Edelmann, R. (1993). *Interpersonal conflicts at work*. Leicester, UK: British Psychological Society.

Egan, G. (1986). *The skilled helper* (3rd edn.). Pacific Grove, CA: Brooks Cole.

Fontana, D. (1989). *Managing stress*. Oxford: Blackwell.

Goleman, D., Boyatzis, R., & McKee, A. (2002). *The new leaders: Transforming the art of leadership into the science of results.* London: Little, Brown.

Goleman, D. (1995) *Emotional intelligence: Why it can matter more than IQ.* London: Bloomsbury.

Parry, G. (1990). *Coping with crises.* Oxford: Blackwell.

Seligman, M. E. P. (1998). *Learned optimism: How to change your mind and your life.* London: Pocket Books.

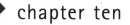

♦ chapter ten

Conflict in Teams

In the frank expression of conflicting opinions lies the greatest promise of wisdom in governmental action.
Louis D. Brandeis (1856–1941)

Washing one's hands of the conflict between the powerful and the powerless means to side with the powerful, not to be neutral.
Paulo Freire

Difficulties are meant to rouse, not discourage. The human spirit is to grow strong by conflict.
William Ellery Channing (1780–1842)

key learning points:

- The organizational causes of team conflicts
- Types of conflict in teams
- How to resolve team conflicts
- Interpersonal conflicts in teams and how to manage them
- How to manage difficult team members

Conflict is not only endemic but, if it is constructive, desirable in teams (Deutsch, 1973). Constructive team conflict can be a source of excellence, quality, and creativity. At the same time we know that conflict in teams can be interpersonally destructive and lead to poor team performance or the breakup of the team altogether (De Dreu & Van de Vliert, 1997), especially where the conflict takes on a personal quality. Although job insecurity or work overload can be major causes of stress, it is often the conflicts with colleagues that keep us awake at night (Romanov, Appelberg, Honkasalo, & Koskenvuo, 1996). Why do these occur and what can we do to prevent or overcome them?

◆ Types of Team Conflict

There are three types of conflict in teams: conflict about the task (e.g., "which new product should we launch"); conflict about team processes (e.g., "It's your job to do that, not mine"); and interpersonal conflict (e.g., "I think you are a rude and irritating person!") (De Dreu & Van Vianen, 2001; Jehn, 1997). In productive and creative teams, constructive task conflict is not only endemic but desirable (Tjosvold, 1998). Team diversity and differences of opinion about how best to meet customers' needs should be a source of excellence, quality, and creativity. *But too much conflict (whether it is about the task or not) or conflict experienced as threatening and unpleasant by team members can destroy relationships and the effectiveness of the team.* What may be a comfortable level of debate for you can be intensely uncomfortable for your colleagues.

Process conflict ("that's your job not mine"; "I have a much heavier workload than she does and it's not fair") and interpersonal conflict undermine team effectiveness and the well-being of team members whatever the level (De Dreu & Van Vianen, 2001). Conflict is especially damaging when it becomes personal, where team members attack one another or denigrate each other's skills, abilities, or performance in some way. This is unhealthy both for the individuals concerned and for the team as a whole. All team members should decisively discourage such conflict and ensure that roles and responsibilities are sufficiently clear and fair.

◆ Resolving Team Conflicts

How do we resolve conflicts? There are five basic ways and only one of them is good. We can *avoid* the conflict. Neither side gets its needs met and the conflict is likely to arise in the future. We can give the other person what they want and *accommodate* them. The consequences are that they get what they want and I don't. I feel resentful and they expect me to accommodate them every time. We can *compete* to win against them at all costs and, if we do, their needs are not met and they are likely to harbor resentment that may manifest in the next conflict. *Compromise* sounds good but it means that neither of us get our needs fully met – still, it is a better solution than the other three. Or we can *collaborate* to find a creative solution that meets both our needs. This is what some call a "win–win" solution. It is the ideal since both parties are happy and their relationship is stronger because of the successful conflict negotiation.

Fisher, Ury, and Patton, in their classic book on negotiating (Fisher et al., 1999), describe four steps involved in principled or ethical negotiation to resolve conflicts. First, separate the people from the problem. We should not get caught up in attributing the problem to the people. Human beings usually explain people's behavior by seeing it as caused by personality rather than by the situation. If you see a parent shouting angrily at their child in the street, you interpret this as an indication of their aggressive personality. It could be that the child has narrowly missed being knocked down, having run into the road, and the parent is angrily berating them as a reaction to parental anxiety. He or she may normally never raise their voice to the child. This error in how we interpret behavior is so deeply ingrained we are unaware of it. Psychologists call it the "fundamental attribution error." It also explains why problems in teams are often, and usually wrongly, attributed to "personality clashes." Focus on the problem that is causing the conflict and be tough on the problem and soft on the people.

Second, focus on interests not on positions. My daughters, Ellie and Rosa, were fighting over the last orange in the fruit bowl, and I "solved" the problem by cutting it in half. Rosa then squeezed her half out to make a juice drink and threw the residue away. Ellie scraped the peel to make zest for a cake she was making, and again, threw the rest in the bin. My "solution" meant that both only got half of what they could have had, if I had taken the time to find out what their underlying interests were rather than their stated positions ("I want the orange"; "No, I want it"). Similarly, in team conflicts we should work out what the underlying interests or needs of the parties are rather than focusing on the stated positions.

Third, invent options for mutual gain. When you are in a conflict, your ability to negotiate and resolve the conflict will be infinitely better if you try to find solutions that meet both parties' interests. This is the opportunity to use your creativity and think of solutions that meet or even exceed what both parties to the conflict are after.

- Determine what are the underlying needs of the parties to the conflict (as opposed to their expressed positions), because conflicts occur when one person's attempts to reach a goal are blocked by another.
- Work with them to find creative solutions that meet or even exceed both party's needs. Do not fall easily back into compromise, and remember that team votes are a way of avoiding rather than dealing directly and satisfactorily with the conflict.

Finally, insist upon objective criteria to ensure the negotiation reaches a fair conclusion, rather than deciding the outcome by force of will. If team members are in conflict over workload, try to find a way of evaluating the solution to show it is fair. For example, if two members of a teaching team are in conflict over how much teaching each should do (a debate about number of contact hours with students and size of classes), work out a standard taking into account both parameters and ensure that both have workloads which are more or less equal using this agreed measure.

◆ Organizational Causes of Conflict

Work role or organization factors are the cause of most interpersonal conflicts in teams. These include:

- Lack of clarity or lack of mutual understanding of roles. This leads to debates about who should do what, suspicions about whether the distribution of workloads is fair, and irritations caused by apparent "interference."
- The absence of clear shared vision and explicit goals. When it is not clear what the task of the team is, there are likely to be conflicts occasioned by competing objectives of team members. One person may want to focus on keeping good records while another may want to innovate, but if the task is not clear, then the conflict is unlikely to be resolved.
- Inadequacy of resources. Trying to provide pensions advice for callers to a help center when the computer system keeps crashing is likely to produce high levels of frustration among team members, which may easily boil over into interpersonal conflict.
- Differences in functional orientation. In the team responsible for providing products for customers in one geographical area the team member responsible for sales focuses on keeping the price of products down and getting the orders filled quickly. The team member responsible for producing the products will be more concerned with producing the product to a high quality and taking the time to do it properly rather than rushing the job and making mistakes. Inevitably they will come into conflict.
- Status inconsistencies. Finance assistant in the team dealing with a senior manager's expenses claims.
- Overlapping authority. It's not clear who is in charge of an aspect of the task.

- Task interdependence. This is where team members have to rely on one another to complete their part of the task successfully. In the construction of a product in cell assembly in manufacturing one team member may be dependent on another to get their part of the production right in order for the next team member to be able to complete their part of the task successfully. Frustrations arise when reliability of a team member is seen to be lower than acceptable (regardless of the cause).
- Incompatible evaluation systems. Quality of product versus speed of delivery versus cost of product.

Case example:

Gwen, a nurse in a primary health care team, was experiencing repeated conflict with the social worker attached to her team. They tended to disagree over cases of suspected nonaccidental injury to children where Gwen felt that the social worker was too ready to involve the courts and the police and too dismissive of Gwen's knowledge of the families involved. The conflict had escalated to the extent that the two had a heated disagreement in Gwen's office that was overheard by other members of staff. Gwen accused the social worker of being unfeeling and too autocratic. The social worker responded by telling Gwen that it was not her job to be doing social work and that she should be looking after the physical health of the family. He called her argumentative, interfering, and noncommunicative and accused her of not being able to work effectively in a team.

In this case, personalities were not at the root of the problem. Rather it was due to a lack of clarity and mutual understanding of roles. There is often conflict between medical and social workers in the community. This is usually because they have not spent time exploring and clarifying each other's roles. The social worker may be unaware of the broader role of the medical worker taking responsibility for all aspects of a family's health and well-being, including the social and emotional aspects. Health workers, on the other hand, often fail to be sufficiently aware of the statutory responsibilities of social workers who ultimately may be accountable in law if a tragic event occurs.

Team members can overcome such conflicts, not by reference to the particular case, but by a full exploration of each other's roles and some negotiation around how the roles can effectively complement rather than compete with one another. Therefore, whenever there is conflict in a team, one of the first things to assess is the extent to which people are clearly aware of each other's roles and the objectives of those roles (Pondy, 1967 offers a useful analysis of conflict processes). An exercise in role negotiation and clarification is described in chapter 4.

 Interpersonal Conflicts

Personality does play an important part in team functioning and in the concept of team roles, as we saw in chapter 2 with the idea that groups of people have "team personalities." Some individuals may be dominant and leader-oriented ("shapers") while others may be more creative (the "plant" team role). Where there are two shapers in a team there may be friction, since two dominant people may well hold opposing views about the team's direction. The monitor-evaluator who is keen to ensure that a decision taken by the team is always right and has been thought through carefully will be unmoved by the enthusiasm and certainty of the creative person in the team. The creative individual may feel irritation at the skeptical questioning and lack of enthusiasm of the monitor-evaluator when a new and potentially exciting proposal is proposed. Some of the differences between team members can be due to characteristic styles of working that, while valuable, may cause mutual antagonism or friction. Recognition of the value of the variability of styles within teams helps to overcome such difficulties.

Managing interpersonal conflicts

There is no doubt, however, that sometimes conflicts between individuals within teams cannot be dismissed as due to role, organizational, or team personality-type factors. Irritations do arise and difficulties do have to be worked through. For the most part people will get on with others with whom they work when that is unavoidable. This is *the psychology of inevitability* – if a child is told that he or she will definitely be sitting next to another particular child in class (whom he or she has not liked previously) over the course of the next year, the child's attitude is likely to change. Similarly if we know we have to work with certain individuals whom we may have found difficult in the past, we may work harder to find strategies to work more effectively and cooperatively with them.

There are four ways of reacting to a difficulty that has occurred with another team member. The first is to be *passive*, which means doing nothing and pretending the problem does not exist, but as indicated above this may have long-term detrimental effects such as simmering frustrations that overflow inappropriately.

The second strategy is to be *passively aggressive*, which is perhaps the most destructive strategy of all. This is where Geoff avoids Laurence, the other team member, doesn't talk to him, deliberately disagrees with every suggestion he makes, denigrates him to colleagues, or even sabotages his work secretly. Such passive-aggressive strategies allow team members no opportunity of reconciling the conflicts or difficulties since they do not involve owning up to the existence of conflict. Passive-aggressive strategies undermine the climate of the whole team and are very destructive to team functioning.

The third approach is to be *aggressive*, attacking the other team member verbally face-to-face with the intention of hurting. Such a strategy is marginally more positive than passive-aggressive or passive approaches since it enables the individual team member to get rid of angry feelings. But it tends to leave a thick residue of bitterness, resentment, and coldness, which harms both team members and the deeper social climate of the team.

The fourth strategy has been called *assertiveness*, which involves telling the other individual about one's own feelings and asking for changes in behavior that might prevent a recurrence of the conflict. Here are illustrations of the difference between aggressive and assertive statements:

- "You're incompetent and you've wasted a whole week's work for me" (aggressive statement).
- "I feel really upset because I relied on you to make sure this information was posted on time. And I feel upset because all my hard work of the week seems wasted" (assertive statement).

Assertiveness therefore involves the clear expression of feelings and the use of "I" rather than "you" statements. It involves being clear about one's own feelings and wants from the situation, whereas aggressive statements simply involve the intention to hurt. Assertive discussions therefore demand that both sides try to use "I" statements in talking about their feelings and in identifying behavior and the consequences of behavior. At the same time, there must be a mutual commitment to identify desired changes in behavior that will prevent the recurrence of the problem.

But when conflicts between team members do arise and cannot be managed in ways so far described, how should team members proceed? Pretending major problems do not exist in a working relationship can be an effective strategy in the short term but the danger is that frustrations build and will erupt in a single destructive incident. Team members should try to work through interpersonal difficulties when they arise, in a constructive open way. This means being clear with the other team member about difficulties and conflicts and setting aside time to talk through them. Avoiding or denying problems is unlikely to make a long-term contribution to team viability. It is clearly best if individual team members can resolve differences with colleagues on a one-to-one basis in an open and constructive way when difficulties first arise. This will be easier in a climate of perceived safety within the team where the development of cliques is positively discouraged.

Team members may have genuine differences (strong political differences for example), but if team members are committed to a shared team vision, and have emotional maturity, they will not allow these differences to interfere with team success. We don't need to vote for the same political party in order to work together successfully to catch a wildebeest. Moreover, there is some evidence that when team leaders intervene to try to resolve interpersonal difficulties between team members, the situation is usually made worse (De Dreu & Van Vianen, 2001). There is nothing wrong with agreeing to differ as long as it does not interfere with the effectiveness of the team.

Where team members are unable to resolve their differences and these are interfering with the team's work, it may be necessary to involve the team leader (or, where the team leader is one of the two protagonists, the team leader's superior). The strategy here should be for the team leader to give each person the opportunity to state his or her feelings about the issue. Once both sides have expressed their feelings, the facts of the case can be addressed. It is important to try to separate out feelings from facts, since the two can become muddled in a discussion that can then lead to further hostility and misunderstanding. By carefully talking through the facts and feelings, the "mediator" can enable both sides to present their cases fully and to explore, perhaps without agreeing on an interpretation of previous events, how future difficulties might be avoided. Mediation, therefore, involves four stages:

- explore the feelings of both team members,
- explore the facts as perceived by both team members,
- agree goals for avoiding a reoccurrence of the conflict,
- agree action plans.

Case example: The retail coordination team

Elaine was the team leader in a retail coordination team of a major oil company. Geoffrey, her newest, youngest, and least-experienced team member, had been with the team for just a year. Elaine then discovered that unknown to her, Geoffrey had been conducting work with a number of retail outlets in a nearby town using the team's resources, at the same time as conducting the major project for which he was employed. When Elaine expressed outrage to Geoffrey, communication broke down.

A meeting was arranged with Petra, the departmental manager, where the initial feelings of both sides were explored and each was given an opportunity to express their frustrations. Elaine was angry since she felt Geoffrey had betrayed her trust by not giving her enough information; she felt she had been misled. Geoffrey expressed his frustration at Elaine not allowing him to proceed with the project when he initially suggested it and felt annoyed that he had to take Elaine's direction over his work.

Petra then encouraged some exploration of the facts of the case, over which there was some disagreement. Geoffrey insisted that he had at one point mentioned the project to Elaine, while Elaine denied this and said that despite weekly meetings with Geoffrey she had never received any information about the fact that he was pursuing the project.

Petra then explored some goals for the future. Both sides agreed on a need to communicate more about all aspects of work, particularly because Geoffrey felt that he did not know enough about what Elaine was doing on a day-to-day basis and felt it was important for him to know as a team member. Both agreed to better communication about all aspects of their work. They set an action plan that involved Geoffrey and Elaine meeting weekly to talk about the progress of the work and to update each other on activities. Geoffrey agreed not to engage in future activities without clear organizational sanction.

A final note of caution: there is sometimes a tendency for team members to wish to hold inquests over every small conflict that takes place within the team. This can have the effect of magnifying those inevitable but small differences that occur between team members on a day-to-day basis. Engaging in such focused, repeated, and concentrated analyses can magnify conflicts and can be as detrimental to team functioning and individual mental health as avoiding discussion of conflicts altogether.

◆ Difficult Team Members

What do you do if there is a particularly difficult member in the team who you feel disrupts the team's work? Your first task is to think carefully about the ways in which this person is difficult and why this person is difficult. Sometimes, when teams are in difficulty, team members can "scapegoat" particular individuals, heaping all the blame for the team's failures on that person, and then trying to drive them away. In this way, they unconsciously try to rid themselves of the problems but are failing to address the real causes (Hackman, 2002).

We often label and treat as difficult people who are different in some way from other team members. The newcomer to a longstanding team, the woman who joins an all-male team, the computer wizard in a team of technophobes, or the Malaysian in a team of Australians are all examples of people who may be stuck with the label "difficult" rather than valuably different. Yet the difference in perspective they offer may save the team from its own homogeneity. Difference can produce creativity, but team members have to value that difference.

Those who disagree with the majority are often labeled "difficult," yet teams with high levels of participation and tolerance of dissent are much more creative and innovative than those that do not tolerate dissent. Think about whether those who are being labeled as "difficult" are simply dissenting and, if so, encourage other team members to explore, value, and be stimulated by their dissenting views. They could well be the most important members of the team. We may also think of team members as "difficult" when we do not understand their role or how they contribute to the team's success. Role clarification and negotiation exercises help solve the problem.

Having considered these possibilities you may conclude that the difficult people are genuinely so. They may be dominating, poor at communicating, aggressive, sarcastic, or gruff. The way to deal with these behavioral problems is to coach, not exclude, the team member. Use coaching skills to help them set targets to improve their interpersonal skills and give feedback on their performance. If possible, encourage the whole team to take responsibility for helping the person to learn to work more effectively as a team member. Encourage, appreciate, shape, and support the team member.

And if you have considered all these options and what you are left with is the recognition that there is someone in the team who does not share the team's core values, then perhaps they should be encouraged to leave the team and find a more suitable place to belong. If the team is committed to helping customers and communicating their respect for clients, yet the team member rigidly sticks to their view that the customers should be deceived or treated with contempt privately, then you should consider how to move them within or out of the organization. Your human resources department can help. Teams are there to do a task (be it catching wildebeest or diagnosing and treating women with breast cancer) and, in the end, should not tolerate stubborn behavior that interferes with their effective performance of the task. But remember that the final example is an unusual situation. It is much more likely that your "difficult" team members are perceived as such because of one or other of the explanations outlined above.

key revision points:

- What are the three types of team conflict and which influence team performance positively or negatively?

- How do you go about resolving conflicts between team members?

- What are the usual organizational causes of team conflicts?

- How should we go about managing interpersonal conflicts between members?

- Why are some team members labeled as difficult and what are the usual causes of this labeling?

- How should you manage difficult team members?

FURTHER READING

De Dreu, C. K. W. & Van de Vliert, E. (eds.) (1997). *Using conflict in organizations*. London: Sage.

Deutsch, M. (1973). *The resolution of conflict: Constructive and destructive processes*. New Haven, CT: Yale University Press.

Jehn, K. (1997). A qualitative analysis of conflict types and dimensions in organizational groups. *Administrative Science Quarterly, 42*, 530–57.

Pondy, L. (1967). Organizational conflict: Concepts and models. *Administrative Science Quarterly, 17*, 296–320.

Tjosvold, D. (1998). Cooperative and competitive goal approaches to conflict: Accomplishments and challenges. *Applied Psychology: An International Review, 47*, 285–342.

West, M. A., Tjosvold, D., & Smith, K. G. (eds.) (2003). *The international handbook of organizational teamwork and cooperative working*. Chichester, UK: Wiley.

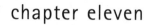
◆ chapter eleven

Teams in Organizations

An empowered organization is one in which individuals have the knowledge, skill, desire, and opportunity to personally succeed in a way that leads to collective organizational success.

Stephen R. Covey

key learning points:

- The six stages of introducing team-based working in organizations

- Types of team communication styles in organizations and their effectiveness

- What support organizations should provide for teams

- The role of the human resource management department

- Reward systems for teams

- What role teams should play in organizations

- A strategy for a team to change the organization

- Interteam relationships and how to improve them.

In this final chapter, we focus on how to build organizations that are structured around teams and can accommodate this diversity and creativity to ensure team and organizational effectiveness. This chapter deals with a question of fundamental importance, largely neglected by researchers, consultants, and managers: *how can we build organizations that ensure the effectiveness of teams as a way of working?*

◆ Introducing Team-based Working (TBW)

The premise of this question is that there is huge unrealized potential of teams and that this is locked away by the failures of organizational leaders to recognize that teams will work only to the extent that the organization is structured around, and values, team working in practice. When teams struggle to function in hierarchical organizations with rigid boundaries between departments, they generally fail (Harris & Beyerlein, 2003; Mohrman, Cohen, & Mohrman, 1995). We must plant the seeds of teamwork in seed beds prepared to nurture and sustain them. Below we describe the six stages involved in developing an organization so that it is structured around teams and ensures their effectiveness (for a detailed account of how to introduce team-based working, along with guides, questionnaires, and practical techniques, see West & Markiewicz, 2003).

1   *Deciding on team-based working (TBW).* The first stage of introducing TBW requires that senior figures understand the value and benefits of team-based working and also that there is a good understanding of the existing structure, culture, and extent of team working in the organization. Senior managers have to be

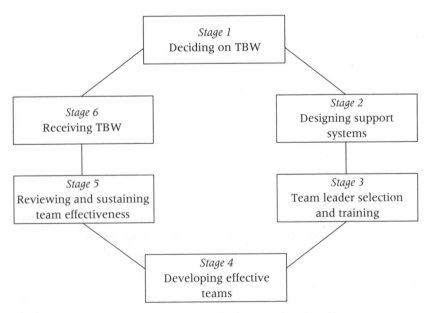

Figure 11.1   The six-stage process of introducing team-based working

committed to the idea of organizing around teams, and those involved in the change process must review what needs to change in the structure and culture of the organization to enable team-based working. The change leaders must then develop a plan for implementing team-based working and have a senior team in place to drive the change forward.

2 *Developing support systems.* This stage requires an examination of support systems relevant to team-based working such as human resource management (HRM) systems, rewards, communication, and training for managers and team members, as well as recruitment and selection practices and making plans to adapt or develop them for TBW. Change leaders will determine what supports need to be in place so that team working can be nourished and spread within the organization. These include:

3 *Team leader and team member selection.* Establish criteria for team leader and team member selection (all employees can help with this), and then select them. Team leaders require training in the necessary knowledge, skills, and abilities, as leading teams is very different from other kinds of leadership. Groups of team leaders can meet regularly to learn together how to be effective in their team leadership, by encouraging the team to share problems, successes, and surprises.

4 *Developing effective teams.* This stage requires understanding and enabling the team development process, which includes clarifying objectives, roles, communication processes, and decision-making processes. The earlier chapters of this book described much of this material.

5 *Reviewing and sustaining team effectiveness.* In this stage, teams are coached to set criteria for the evaluation of team performance and to identify required changes to improve performance. Team leaders must examine performance, innovation, team members' satisfaction, and their learning and skill development, since all are vital areas of team performance.

6 *Reviewing team-based working.* The final stage involves evaluating the contribution of team-based working to the organization's effectiveness and making any necessary changes to ensure the continued and optimal contribution of team-based working to the organization.

These then are the six main stages of introducing TBW but what does the organization look like when the process is complete? Introducing team-based working involves dramatic, deep, and wide-ranging change to the organization's structure and culture. In traditional organizations, there are command structures with status levels representing points in the hierarchy – supervisors, managers, senior managers, assistant chief executives, and so on. In team-based organizations, the structures are collective. Teams orbit around the top management team and other senior teams (which themselves model good teamwork), influencing and being influenced, rather than being directed or directive. The gravitational or inspirational force of different teams affects the performance of the teams around them. The traditional organization has a chart with lines of reporting and layers of hierarchy but the team-based organization looks more like a solar system with planets revolving around each other and affected by the central force of the major planet (the top management team). The role of team leaders is to ensure that their teams work as powerful and effective parts of that solar system and that they think about how the system as a whole works, not just their particular planets. To do this they must continually emphasize integration and cooperation between teams. I suggest that team leaders keep asking leaders of those other teams they most work with, "How can we help each other more?", "What are we doing that gets in the way of your effectiveness?" and "Can we work together to come up with a radical new way of improving our services for customers?"

In traditional organizations, managers manage and control; whereas the role of the team leader in team-based organizations is to encourage teams in their organizations to be largely self-managing and take responsibility for monitoring the effectiveness of their strategies and processes. In one company I worked in, a production team videoed their performance in the production process and invited members of other teams to view the video and suggest ways in which they could dramatically improve the production process. This led to radical improvements in productivity, quality, and time taken for goods to reach the customers.

Organizational objectives, customer service, innovation and team working are the leadership mantras in team-based organizations.

◆ The Relationship Between Teams and Their Organizations

Deborah Ancona and David Caldwell (Ancona & Caldwell, 1992) explored how teams "bridge the boundaries," that is, how teams interact with their organizations as a whole. By studying teams interacting with their organizations, Ancona and Caldwell identified three main strategies that teams use in managing their organizational environments:

Ambassadorial activities: these involve communicating with and influencing senior management in order to promote the team's profile and to give senior management a picture of the team as effective, committed, and innovative. The aim of ambassadorial activities is also to secure organizational resources and protect the team from excessive interference.

Task coordinator activities: these aim at improving communication with other teams and departments. Rather than being characterized by vertical communication (as is the case with ambassadorial activity), task coordinator activities focus on coordination, negotiation, and feedback horizontally, that is, with departments and teams at the same organizational level. The aim is to manage workflow activities in a coordinated way through negotiation and via feedback with other departments and teams, in order to achieve effective performance.

In the case of, say, an oil company training team this would mean engaging in high levels of communication with functional departments in order to gain information about training needs. The training team would also negotiate with those other departments in order to specify training course prices, priorities, and frequencies. By seeking constant feedback on the adequacy of the training they would also be in a better position to coordinate and negotiate in the future.

Scouting activities: these aim to provide the group with up-to-date information on market needs and requirements and on new technical developments. The aim of scouting activities is to be aware of changes occurring in the external environment of the team. One example comes from a research team established to examine the factors that contributed to the performance of manufacturing firms. One team member contacted other researchers on a regular basis to find out about new developments in the area, perused relevant journals to glean information about new methodologies, and consulted with academic contacts about related research. Such scouting activities provide a means of ensuring that a team is up to date with technical developments. This same team member also consulted with senior managers in other similar organizations to discover their principal questions about company performance in order to identify correctly market needs for the research.

Not all teams have a single dominant strategy for external activity within the organization. Some employ all three types of activities, while others focus on only one. Still others are isolationist, employing none of the strategies in any consistent way. Ancona and Caldwell found that team performance was not dependent upon the *level* of organizational communication that teams maintained. Far more important was the *type* of activities they engaged in. Ancona and Caldwell found that teams that engaged predominantly in scouting activities had poorer performance than other teams. Moreover, internal processes within the team tended to be unsatisfactory. Task and team cohesiveness were both lowest in teams that adopted predominantly scouting activity strategies. In contrast, teams that adopted a "comprehensive strategy" of a mix of ambassadorial, task coordinator, and scouting activities tended to have the highest performance, task process, and team cohesiveness scores.

In the short term, ambassadorial activities were associated with the best team performance, good task processes, and high cohesiveness. But over the long term, a combination of ambassadorial and task coordinator external activities appears best. Comprehensive strategy teams were the most effective overall, though they seemed to pay a price with low team cohesiveness compared with the pure ambassadorial strategy teams.

Isolationist teams tended to do badly, though, unlike the scouting teams, they did have higher scores on internal task processes and cohesiveness. It may be that these teams concentrated so much on internal processes that they neglected important organizational cues and so performed less well. Teams that engaged predominantly in scouting seemed to make their work so complex that they were unable to perform effectively. By constantly seeking new approaches, they were unable to adopt a single team plan that took them forward over any period. They could not make clear decisions about work plans or processes and could not implement a plan. Continual exploration brought conflicting information, requiring complex internal interaction. As the difficulty of decision making became greater, relationships within the teams suffered.

This research shows that, contrary to popular belief, it is not the amount of external communication that a team engages in that predicts successful team performance. Rather it is the *type* of external communication.

◆ What do Teams Need from Their Organizations?

Hackman and his colleagues (Hackman, 1990) have concluded that there are six principal areas within which teams need organizational support: targets, resources, information, education, feedback, and technical/process assistance in functioning. Examining the extent to which organizations provide team support in these areas can help in discovering the underlying causes of team difficulties.

Targets

Teams need support from an organization in determining targets or objectives. Surprisingly few teams receive clear targets from their organizations, often because organizational targets and aims are not sufficiently clear. It is striking, when team members try to outline their objectives and team targets, how few have clear notions of what is required of them. The implication is that teams should derive their targets and objectives by scrutinizing organizational objectives or mission statements. These are often such vague good intentions or abstract sentiments however, that it is almost impossible for a team to derive clear targets. Where, through a process of negotiation, teams are able to determine their targets in consultation and collaboration with those hierarchically above them, there is usually a better level of performance.

Resources

The organization is required to provide adequate resources to enable the team to achieve its targets or objectives. Resources include having the right number and skill mix of people; adequate financial resources to enable effective functioning; secretarial or administrative support; adequate accommodation; and adequate technical assistance and support (such as computers, blood pressure testing equipment, or whatever technologies are required for the team to be successful).

Information

Teams need information from the organization that will enable them to achieve their targets and objectives. If teams are not told about changes in strategy or policy they will not function effectively. Ensuring that relevant information reaches a team to enable it to perform effectively is an essential component of an organization's management. For example, an oil company that decides to develop large numbers of international teams with team members based in different countries has to communicate these plans to its training department in order that they can implement training for cross-cultural teams.

Education

Part of an organization's responsibilities for effective team functioning is to provide the appropriate levels and content of education for staff within teams. The purpose of such training and education is to enable team members to contribute most effectively to team functioning and to develop as individuals. This includes on-the-job training, coaching via supervisor, and training courses including residential training courses or distance learning courses. There should be adequate access to training that is relevant to the team's work and of a sufficient quality and quantity to enable them to perform to maximum effectiveness.

Feedback

Teams require timely and appropriate organizational feedback on their performance if they are to function effectively. Timely feedback means that it occurs as soon as possible after the team has performed its task, or occurs sufficiently regularly to enable the team to correct inappropriate practices or procedures. Appropriate feedback means that it is accurate and gives a clear picture of team performance.

For some teams it is difficult to gain accurate feedback. For a football team, feedback is immediate and is not dependent upon an organization, that is, match results are evident on a weekly basis. For a team responsible for providing training in one division of, say, a major oil company, organizational feedback might take the form of senior managers' satisfaction with improved performance. This could include measuring the results from technical training courses in customer service in retail outlets (i.e., filling stations). Such information could come from surveys of customer satisfaction with retail operators' services. Organizations should aim to improve continuously in the extent to which they provide useful, accurate, and timely feedback.

Technical and process assistance

Teams need their organizations to provide the specialized knowledge and support that will enable them to perform their work effectively. A primary health care team engaged in developing its practice objectives, by identifying the health needs of the practice population, might need the health authority to deploy a community medical officer to advise the team on patterns in local health and ill-health. For a training team in an oil company, technical assistance might take the form of specialist computing experts and marketing strategists, advising the company on how to communicate most effectively to managers throughout Europe, in order to market their training courses to managers in different functions.

Process assistance refers to the organizational help available when the team encounters team process problems. There needs to be someone in the organization (or an external consultant) who can assist teams when they have difficulties they cannot seem to solve. All team leaders should see this as a normal activity – "it's like visiting the doctor when you have an illness; teams too need expert help from time to time."

◆ The Role of Human Resource Management (HRM)

In order to provide the supports that are necessary for team effectiveness, the HRM department of organizations must play a powerful role. They need to develop support systems to ensure the success of team-based working by taking the following steps. HR managers must develop their knowledge about all aspects of team working, including team composition, team development, team processes, team performance management, and particularly, interteam conflict and how to manage it. They should visit five or six outstanding examples of team-based organizations to learn about good practice and to share their learning with everyone in the organization. The teams need clear constructive feedback and they should help teams set goals and give feedback on the team's performance in relation to four areas:

1   The team's performance, be it producing parts, treating patients, or providing customer service – likely to be best defined and evaluated by the "customers" of the teams.
2   Team member growth and well-being – the learning, development, and satisfaction of team members.
3   Team innovation is almost the best barometer of team functioning. Teams should be fountains of creativity.
4   Interteam relations – cooperation with other teams and departments within the organization.

The HRM department must make sure that the reward systems reward teamwork as well as individual performance. Most important is for them to check annually whether team members see the reward system as transparent, just, and motivating (see Box 11.1 for more detailed advice on reward systems).

When selecting new staff the HRM department should help team members take account of previous experience of applicants in working in teams, team-working competencies, and the motivation to work in teams. Where team members manage their own selection, HR and an external participant can ensure probity and an alternative view so that team members do not simply select clones of themselves. The HR department should provide training for team members in how to work in teams (not just team-building events), and training for team managers and for internal consultants working with teams. Both new and experienced team managers will also benefit from the support of a mentor. This may be a manager from another level of the organization or a team manager from another team who has experience of working with teams.

The HR department should use extensive communication devices to ensure everyone in the teams is clear about the purpose of the organization, its performance, and the importance of teamwork. They can use regular emails, newsletters, conversations, rewards, and even press releases to newspapers to communicate about successes. Moreover, they and managers should give quick, public, and positive recognition to accomplishments of the teams and their members whenever possible.

Putting these systems in place means that teamwork is nourished and supported in the organization rather than hanging by threads. Team members will be motivated; the organization will become healthier; and the roles of team leaders will be challenging, interesting, and rewarding, since they will not always be dealing with the problems created by lack of support for teamwork.

◆ What do Organizations Require from Teams?

Organizations need teams *to set and then achieve objectives* that enable the organization to achieve its own targets and goals. A health organization, for example, will require their primary health care teams to meet the health needs of the local population. The training team in an oil company, on the other hand, may be required to identify carefully training needs and respond to them strategically in order that the organization can achieve its overall objectives via the improved individual performance of employees.

Box 11.1: Developing team reward systems

Reward processes make it possible to appraise and reward people on the basis both of the results they achieve and the extent to which their work promotes innovation, quality, team working, and continual improvement. Reward processes demonstrate the organization's commitment to those values. Reward systems must therefore be open and clearly understood by all involved (Parker, McAdams, & Zielinski, 2000). The focus of reward systems can include:

The individual team member

Here individual performance is appraised and rewarded. This can include individual rewards for contribution to team working where this is a specific target set for the individual. Performance-related pay can reflect individual contributions to the team's performance as rated by other team members.

The team

Here reward is related to the achievement of predetermined team goals. Reward may be distributed equally to each member of the team or it may be apportioned by senior management, by the team leader, or in a manner determined by the team itself. It is important to note that where rewards are given equally to team members by an external party, this can lead to considerable resentment. Team members who do not pull their weight are seen as "free riders" and their failures lead to resentment and demotivation among other team members. This will be exacerbated if the distribution of team rewards is achieved in ways that do not mirror the effort or contribution made by individual team members. It is important therefore that the reward system for the team is seen as fair by team members, and this may involve some process by which team members themselves determine the distribution of the team rewards.

The organization

The performance of either the total organization or the business unit is reflected in rewards allocated to individuals or

Box 11.1: (cont'd)

teams. Incorporating all elements (individual, team, and organizational) provides a well-rounded reward system. In team-based organizations there must be a strong emphasis on team performance and as much delegation of decisions regarding team reward distribution as possible.

The keys to successful reward systems are:

- clear, achievable, but challenging targets which team members understand, agree, and ideally are involved in setting;
- clear and fair means of measuring team outcomes;
- team members working interdependently to achieve team goals;
- allowing the team a considerable degree of autonomy in the way in which it manages its work;
- giving the team access to the necessary materials, skills, and knowledge to achieve the task;
- defining a reward valuable enough to be worth having, and delivered soon after the achievement of the outcome.

How can organizations go about designing systems for rewarding teams while still rewarding individuals? Reward schemes should emphasize the core value of teamwork, and this needs driving home repeatedly. Many managers make the mistake of assuming that employees understand the organization's core values. They need to be repeatedly affirmed and spelled out. Managers should also strive to tell employees how they are performing continually (by providing mostly positive feedback) and to reinforce the messages about how the rewards link to the core values of the organization.

It also makes sense to create a smorgasbord of reward plans. Merck (a US company), for example, has an organizational level incentive that pays rewards to employees for the achievement of annual organizational targets. This is augmented by a system whereby team members nominate each other for outstanding team performance, which earns nonmonetary rewards. For high performing teams there is a quarterly stock option reward plan. Another company (ASCAP) allows all

Box 11.1: (*cont'd*)

account services teams that meet their targets to receive an award that represents a percentage of the individual's base pay. In addition, there is a sales team of the year ceremony to which all teams that exceed their annual targets are invited. Although only one team wins the big award, all the other teams receive a plaque and merchandise in recognition of their achievement.

Of course, all this means that senior managers have to budget for recognition activities in advance and to make sure there is sufficient resource to ensure the systems really have an impact. That also means planning to collect, process, and feedback performance data. Those data must be of high quality and perceived to be reliable and valid by employees. The rewards must also be sufficiently substantial to matter to the employees, since the value of payoffs are in the eye of the beholder. Some organizations offer a variety of rewards from which employees can choose: travel passes, money, a case of wine, time off with pay, flexitime working, and so on. Employees can then choose rewards that are most valuable to them.

Cooperation between teams is required by organizations, even when they are competing for office space, resources, or staff. Competing teams may deliberately deceive one another or try to hamper one another's performance. When teams cooperate within organizations, not only is the organization more likely to achieve its objectives, but individual team performance is also improved. Competition between teams within organizations generally results in poor organizational performance (West, Tjosvold, & Smith, 2003).

An increasingly common phenomenon within organizations is the use of *cross-functional teams*. These are combinations of people from different teams who come together to improve communication and decision making. For example, in a company that manufactures springs for the automotive industry, cross-functional groups may draw individuals from production, marketing, sales, and customer liaison in order to identify and overcome quality and performance problems. Such cross-functional groups can address quality problems and ensure cross-team communication, coordination, and cooperation. Such cross-team collaboration and communication fosters high levels of creativity and innovation within organizational settings.

Organizations also need teams to be *agents of innovation, change, and even revolution*. So far we have considered teams as though their objectives and those of the organization are consistent rather than in conflict. But sometimes an organization's objectives and those of a team may not be consistent. A surgical team may feel that the managerial emphasis on cost cutting and reduction of waiting list times has jeopardized the quality of care available to patients. The management group, in contrast, may argue for the importance of setting priorities in treatment, since they have a limited budget with which to provide surgical care. The oil company training team may oppose senior management's strategy of "macho" management that emphasizes increasing employee insecurity, while imposing compulsory redundancies and new contracts. The training team, in conjunction with personnel, may wish to oppose this policy and bring about organizational change. How is this to be done?

In chapter 7, the literature on "minority influence" was examined and this showed how minorities, by being persistent and consistent in the face of opposition, can bring about a subtle conversion of attitudes among majorities. This research has demonstrated convincingly how a well-organized minority may alter the thinking of a majority. The research also helps to partly explain how groups that start out as minorities, such as feminist or ecological movements, subsequently may bring about shifts in thinking, behavior, and even national policies. Serge Moscovici, who pioneered research and theory in this area, has argued that innovation can only come about through the conflict created by minority influence (Moscovici, Mugny, & van Avermaet, 1985). How can a team draw on this understanding in order to change organizational objectives and strategy?

1   *The team must have a clear vision of what it wishes to achieve.* For example, a personnel department might have developed a major commitment to the implementation of equal opportunities on a real rather than cosmetic organizational basis. Opposition from senior management may exist, but as long as the team has a shared vision of equal opportunities for women, ethnic minority groups, and the disabled, they have a chance of success. In order to be effective and to sustain minority influence, the vision must be one that motivates and inspires team members – a future they really feel is worth fighting for.

2   *The vision must be clearly articulated and coherently expressed.* In order to be effective, minorities must put across a clear consistent message backed up by convincing underlying arguments. A team in which the minority vision is unanimously held and consistently argued for is many times more effective than an individual working alone – indeed it is exponentially more effective. Team members must present the same vision and the same arguments in favor of the vision. Where disagreement exists among members of a minority group they are not so effective in influencing the views of the majority and bringing about real change.

3   *They must be flexible in responding to the views of others.* Minorities that are perceived to be radical and inflexible tend to be rejected by the majority as too extreme to bargain with. It is important for a minority to appear willing to listen to the views of others and make modifications to their proposals, while not fundamentally distorting their vision. The personnel department has to be prepared to listen to senior managers who argue that, say, introducing large numbers of untrained people very quickly into the organization may have a detrimental effect upon performance, or that any equal opportunities strategy should be managed in stages. Failure to respond to apparently reasonable arguments can cause the minority to be dismissed. This should not involve a team compromising its fundamental objectives.

4   *Persistence is essential.* For a team to bring about organizational change it must be persistent. Minority movements such as the feminists and ecological campaigns had influence partly because of the repeated presentation of the same coherent message and the same arguments. Minority influence occurs because of persistent communication. Where a team is defeated in a committee or in some managerial decision-making process, it should not give up but should maintain its stance and either go back to the same decision-making bodies or find alternative routes to influence the organization. Presenting the same message persistently across the organization is likely to have the effect of water dripping on a stone: eventually the stone will wear away. In short, the message is: *prepare, rehearse, present, and present again.* In other words, the vision and arguments for the team's position should be prepared and rehearsed in private and then the team should repeatedly present its approach to people throughout the organization. *Don't give up!*

5   *Participation*: The single best way of reducing resistance to change is by involving people in the change process (Heller, Pusić, Strauss,

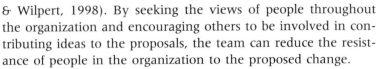

& Wilpert, 1998). By seeking the views of people throughout the organization and encouraging others to be involved in contributing ideas to the proposals, the team can reduce the resistance of people in the organization to the proposed change.

6   *The bad news*: An inevitable consequence of acting as an agent for revolutionary change is that the team increases organizational conflict. Repeatedly challenging organizational objectives or practices inevitably provokes conflict, often with people in higher status positions who have greater power. This is very threatening and deters many teams from engaging in revolutionary change processes. If a vision is worth fighting for, however, then team members will be prepared for the conflict that ensues. Such revolutionary approaches to organizational change also bring with them unpopularity. The majority in organizations tend to conform because it makes for a more peaceful life. Those who introduce conflict are likely to become unpopular since they raise anxiety. Again, if the vision is important to a team – for example, in the case of a hospital nursing team, improving the quality of health of those in their care – team members may be prepared to tolerate unpopularity or even job insecurity as the price they pay to achieve their vision of a better world. *Individuals should not try to implement this strategy for change alone since the research evidence suggests they are likely to fail and possibly to suffer. It is a group strategy for change.*

Such revolutionary teams may seem a threat to organizations. There is good reason for supposing that organizations that have no revolutionary teams are stagnant however, since conformity processes have dampened down the fiery forces for change, conflict, and innovation. Organizations need revolutionary teams just as they need people with vision. Heat is often produced through the friction created by sharply differing views within organizations, and this heat can then fire creative and innovative processes.

Teams within organizations are required to meet objectives that further organizational aims. In order to do this they need organizational support and resources such as information, training, accommodation, equipment, and managerial support. But organizations are political entities characterized by conflicting interests, goals, and agendas, and teams must manage this environment effectively in order to survive. They must develop strategies that raise the team's profile with senior management and win resources, that coordinate their efforts with those of other teams and departments, and that monitor the environment to ensure they are up to date with "market needs" and new technical developments.

To ensure long-term effectiveness, all teams should develop and sustain an evolutionary approach to their work, especially in changeable uncertain environments. This involves regular reflection on the team's work and purpose, along with appropriate modification of activities and aims. Ultimately, team success and effectiveness is constrained or enhanced by the team's collective intelligence and integrity in its dealings with the wider organization.

 Bridging Across Teams

The strengths of team working in organizations are the involvement of all in contributing their skills and knowledge, in good collective decision making, and innovation. The fundamental weakness is the tendency of team-based organizations to be torn and damaged by competition, hostility, and rivalry between teams.

Early research in social psychology, such as the famous Robber's Cave studies (see Box 11.2), showed how psychological group identification occurs almost immediately when people are randomly assigned to groups, with dramatic behavioral consequences of strong group loyalty and in-group favoritism (Sherif, Harvey, White, Hood, & Sherif, 1961). People develop group identification with the most minimal social cues (Billig & Tajfel, 1973; Tajfel, 1970; Tajfel & Billig, 1974). The tendency of people to discriminate in favor of their own group and to discriminate against members of out-groups is pervasive (Brewer, 2001; Turner, 1985). Moreover this in-group favoritism occurs spontaneously and without obvious value to the individual. Research indicates that there is no need for material advantage to the self or inferred similarity to other group members for group identification to occur. There is evidence that external threats lead to the creation of firmer bonds within groups (Stein, 1976) while at the same time increasing the threat of rejection to deviants (Lauderdale, Smith-Cunnien, Parker, & Inverarity, 1984). Groups clearly seek solidarity when confronted by external threat.

The tendency of people to discriminate in favor of their own group is what we all do and is at the root of many of the most horrific conflicts in our world. It does not matter whether it is about football teams, gender, race, function (sales, production), or the other work team. The role of team leaders is to understand and recognize this tendency and take action to prevent, reduce, or overcome it.

Box 11.2: The Robber's Cave studies

TEAMWORK IN PRACTICE

Sherif and his colleagues carried out three large studies of boys in typical American summer camps in Robber's Cave State Park, Oklahoma (Sherif et al., 1961). The design involved three stages of group formation, intergroup conflict, and conflict reduction. Initially, boys from well-to-do backgrounds, aged around 12 years, were assigned to one of two groups, each around 10 or 11 children in size. They had little contact with the other group, playing or working in different locations. The groups developed their own cultures, norms, nicknames, and symbols.

In the second stage, a series of intergroup competitions was announced, with the winning group to receive a set of gleaming penknives and the other group nothing. Whereas in the first phase, the groups had coexisted quite happily, they now developed intense dislike and hostility and, on some occasions, even attacked each other physically. There was considerable "in-group" bias and "out-group" prejudice, with the boys exaggerating the effectiveness and success of their own group, and developing discriminatory and derogatory attitudes to the other group. Their leadership changed hands to a more aggressive individual. In some of the studies, the boys' existing best friends had initially been assigned to the other groups, but during this conflict stage 90 percent of them chose boys from within their own groups.

In the third and final phase, the experimenters tried to reduce intergroup conflict by creating "superordinate goals." For example, they arranged for the camp truck to break down several miles from camp, requiring both groups to pull the truck using a tug-of-war rope to get it "jump started" and back to camp for lunch. Similar manipulations, which introduced superordinate goals (the groups shared an overall goal that eclipsed their immediate within-group goals), led to a reduction in intergroup conflict and hostility. Similar results have emerged from many studies of intergroup behavior regardless of the age or gender of participants. They point to the fundamental nature of human intergroup conflict and the need to develop methods for avoiding it (see Brown, 2000).

These biases against other teams include attitudes in the form of prejudice ("when an order is not completed properly it's always the result of the sales people not getting accurate information in the first place, not us in production"); thoughts in the form of stereotyping ("the sales department are all greedy individualists"); and behavior (refusing to give information to the sales department about the likely date of completion of an order). Threats (or perceived threats) between teams are at the root of much anxiety and anger within organizations that must not be allowed to persist. The hierarchy of threat ranges from threats to the team's social identity (male managers being threatened by the increase in numbers of female managers in a top management team); through threats to their goals and values (doctors perceiving hospital managers forcing them to consider resources alongside quality of patient care); position in the hierarchy (doctors perceiving managers as threatening their authority); to the group's very existence (doctors seeing nurse practitioners as a threat to their own existence). Such threats can be realistic, as in the battle between departments for scarce resources, or symbolic when values or norms are threatened (Hewstone, Rubin, & Willis, 2002).

Leaders should deal with these problems between teams by directly addressing the issue. First, they should explain to team members that this hostility across team boundaries is a natural human tendency and that it can be overcome. Second, they should encourage team members to recognize that they have to learn to cooperate with and support other teams – that is in their best interests, as well as that of the organization and the customers. If there are legitimate grievances between the teams, these must be dealt with in a way that both sides see as just. Team leaders can hold meetings between themselves or between the teams to find solutions that both teams see as just.

Leaders have to be alert as to which team or department their members tend to speak negatively about, and should not buy into the conversation. They have to assert that it may not be fair for them to talk about the other team in this way and suggest ways of addressing and solving the problems that cause them to be negative in their comments. That is one of the lonely parts of the team leader's role.

In my local residential area, social and health care workers have been subsumed within a new Community and Health Action Group, rather than continuing to work in separate organizations. As a result, they are learning to work together and avoid overlaps and contradictory advice in providing for people in the local community. Conflicts are being resolved creatively rather than smoldering, and the result is much better service and support for people, and less anxiety and anger across the health and social care boundaries. Team managers have encouraged this by getting team members to identify the valuable differences between the services provided by their own and the other team. As the groups cooperate, it has become clear to both that they should maintain their separate roles but work together. Both sides bring complementary and much needed skills to the task and need to work together and support each other.

Other practical techniques to use include:

- *Team-member exchanges*: Team members can work for a period in other teams, or visit as observers in order to increase mutual understanding and provide opportunities for individual development.
- *Publicizing team news*: Internal organization newsletters are a forum for providing information about the successes of good interteam working cooperation and support.
- *Benchmarking*: When teams discover new ways of working, or solutions to old problems, they should communicate them to all other teams so they can take advantage of the breakthrough. When team leaders use their positions to encourage this, they build an expectation that it is proper to share best practice and reduce unhealthy competition to be the best team.

◆ Conclusions

Four themes have repeatedly emerged in this book, intersecting to form a single repeated pattern. First, in today's highly uncertain organizations, characterized by high levels of work demands and rapidly changing structures and cultures, we can enhance performance by team members taking time away to reflect quietly upon their functioning. This allows them to adapt courageously in order to achieve new evolutionary forms that fit their circumstances better. Secondly, teams need to find creative ways of working that challenge existing orthodoxies and offer alternatives to the status quo if they are to contribute substantially to organizational and societal development. Such creativity only comes from constructive conflict, and a preparedness to tolerate and even encourage uncertainty and ambiguity. In this way, those who work in teams can experience the excitement and mutual appreciation generated by real breakthroughs because of human collaboration. Thirdly, in demanding, changing, and uncertain environments people must support one another to create climates of safety, confidence, and empowerment. Fourth, teams exist within

organizations that will either provide nourishing and stimulating environments or prove anoxic and starve them of the means of survival.
People form teams, and we must understand the human issues involved
in teamwork. If the team is to dance creatively and in synchrony,
they have to practice and reflect, practice and reflect.

If the motivation and commitment of people are to be engaged in
the work of their teams, there must be a strong sense of the value
of the work they do. This may be in promoting health, conserving
the environment, helping others to learn, supporting those in need,
producing high quality goods for people, ensuring safety, promoting
understanding, confronting injustice, or contributing to the community.
Vision is derived from values and our values determine our motivation. Reflexivity helps to clarify for team members the values they
hold about both team social functioning and task performance. Such
focus and clarity may also make salient the differences between team
members' views and those of senior management or the organization
as a whole. This in turn may lead to conflict. But such conflict is
necessary for organizational adaptability, and successful innovation
ensures that organizations reflect rather than eclipse the diversity of
values in society. Through the development of the evolutionary and
revolutionary reflective teams described throughout this book, organizations may better serve the societies of which they are a part.

key revision points:

- What are the six stages of introducing team-based
  working and what are the tasks of each stage?

- What are the three patterns of external communication
  in teams and which combinations best promote team
  effectiveness and cohesiveness?

- What six sources of support do teams need from their
  organizations?

- Describe the role of the HRM department in developing
  team-based working

- What reward systems will be best for team-based
  organizations?

- What methods can leaders employ to reduce interteam
  and interdepartmental hostility in their organizations?

FURTHER READING

Hackman, J. R. (1990). *Groups that work (and those that don't)*. San Francisco: Jossey-Bass.

Harris, C. & Beyerlein, M. M. (2003). Team-based organization: Creating an environment for team success. In M. A. West, D. Tjosvold, & K. G. Smith (eds.), *Handbook of organizational teamwork and cooperative working* (pp. 187–210). Chichester, UK: Wiley.

Hewstone, M., Rubin, M., & Willis, H. (2002). Intergroup bias. *Annual Reviews of Psychology, 53*, 575–604.

Mohrman, S., Cohen, S., & Mohrman, L. (1995). *Designing team based organizations*. London: Jossey Bass.

Parker, G., McAdams, J., & Zielinski, D. (2000). *Rewarding teams: Lessons from the trenches*. San Francisco, CA: Jossey Bass.

Tajfel, H. (1970). Experiments in intergroup discrimination. *Scientific American, 223*, 96–102.

West, M. A. & Markiewicz, L. (2003). *Building team-based working*. Oxford: Blackwell.

West, M. A., Tjosvold, D., & Smith, K. G. (eds.) (2003). *The international handbook of organizational teamwork and cooperative working*. Chichester, UK: Wiley.

Bibliography

Agarwal, R. (2003). Teamwork in the netcentric organization. In M. A. West, D. Tjosvold, & K. G. Smith (eds.), *International handbook of organizational teamwork and cooperative working* (pp. 443–62). Chichester, UK: Wiley.

Ainsworth, M. D. S. (1982). Attachment: Retrospect and prospect. In C. M. Parkes & J. Stevenson-Hinde (eds.), *The place of attachment in human behavior* (pp. 3–30). New York: Basic Books.

Amabile, T. M. (1997). Motivating creativity in organizations: On doing what you love and loving what you do. *California Management Review, 40,* 39–58.

Ancona, D. F. & Caldwell, D. F. (1992). Bridging the boundary: External activity and performance in organizational teams. *Administrative Science Quarterly, 37,* 634–65.

Anderson, N. & West, M. A. (1994). *The team climate inventory: Manual and user's guide.* Windsor, UK: ASE Press.

Anderson, N. & West, M. A. (1998). Measuring climate for work group innovation: Development and validation of the Team Climate Inventory. *Journal of Organizational Behavior, 19,* 235–58.

Anderson, N. R. & Sleap, S. (in press). An evaluation of gender differences on the Belbin team role self-perception inventory. *Journal of Organizational Behavior.*

Anderson, N. R. & Thomas, H. D. C. (1996). Work group socialization. In M. A. West (ed.), *The handbook of work group psychology* (pp. 423–50). Chichester, UK: Wiley.

Andrews, F. M. (ed). (1979). *Scientific productivity.* Cambridge, UK: Cambridge University Press.

Applebaum, E. & Batt, R. (1994). *The new American workplace.* Ithaca, NY: ILR Press.

Argyris, C. (1978). *Organizational learning: A theory of action perspective.* Reading, MA: Addison Wesley.

Argyris, C. (1990). *Overcoming organizational defences: Facilitating organizational learning.* Boston, MA: Allyn and Bacon.

Argyris, C. (1993). *Knowledge for action: A guide to overcoming barriers to organizational change.* San Francisco: Jossey Bass.

Asch, S. E. (1956). Studies of independence and conformity: 1. A minority of one against a unanimous majority. *Psychological Monographs, 70(a)*, 1–70.

Ashford, S. J. & Tsui, A. S. (1991). Self regulation for managerial effectiveness: The role of active feedback seeking. *Academy of Management Journal, 34*, 251–80.

Barchas, P. (1986). A sociophysiological orientation to small groups. In E. Lawler (ed.), *Advances in group processes* (vol. 3, pp. 209–46). Greenwich, CT: JAI Press.

Barrick, M. R. & Mount, M. K. (1991). The big five personality dimensions and job performance: A meta-analysis. *Personnel Psychology, 44*, 1–26.

Barrick, M. R., Stewart, G. L., Neubert, M. J., & Mount, M. K. (1998). Relating member ability and personality to work-team processes and team effectiveness. *Journal of Applied Psychology, 83*, 377–91.

Barsade, S. & Gibson, D. E. (1998). Group emotion: A view from the top and bottom. In D. Gruenfeld et al. (eds.), *Research on managing groups and teams* (pp. 81–102). Greenwich, CT: JAI press.

Bass, B. (1990). *Bass & Stogdill's handbook of leadership: Theory, research and managerial applications* (3rd edn.). New York: Free Press.

Baumeister, R. F. & Leary, M. R. (1995). The need to belong: Desire for interpersonal attachments as a fundamental human motivation. *Psychological Bulletin, 117*, 497–529.

Baumeister, R. F., Wotman, S. R., & Stillwell, A. M. (1993). Unrequited love: On heartbreak, anger, guilt, scriptlessness and humiliation. *Journal of Personality and Social Psychology, 64*, 377–94.

Belbin, R. M. (1981). *Management teams: Why they succeed or fail.* London: Heinemann.

Belbin, R. M. (1993). *Team roles at work: A strategy for human resource management.* Oxford: Butterworth, Heinemann.

Billig, M. & Tajfel, H. (1973). Social categorization and similarity in intergroup behavior. *European Journal of Social Psychology, 3*, 27–51.

Bond, R. & Smith, P. B. (1996). Culture and conformity: A meta-analysis of studies using Asch's (1952b, 1956) line judgement task. *Psychological Bulletin, 119*, 111–37.

Borrill, C., West, M. A., Shapiro, D., & Rees, A. (2000). Team working and effectiveness in health care. *British Journal of Health Care, 6(8)*, 364–71.

Brewer, M. B. (2001). Ingroup identification and intergroup conflict: When does ingroup love become outgroup hate? In R. Ashmore, L. Jussim, & D. Wilder (eds.), *Social identity, intergroup conflict, and conflict reduction.* New York: Oxford University Press.

Brodbeck, F. C., Lee, N., & Overend, J. (2003). Ethnical diversity and group performance in a business simulation exercise: A matter of time and scale. Paper presented at the European Association of Work and Organisational Psychology (EAWOP), Lisbon, May 2003.

Brown, R. (2000). *Group processes* (2nd edn.). Oxford, UK: Blackwell.

Byrne, D. (1971). *The attraction paradigm.* New York: Academic Press.

Campion, M. A., Medsker, G. J., & Higgs, A. C. (1993). Relations between work group characteristics and effectiveness: Implications for designing effective work groups. *Personnel Psychology, 46*, 823–50.

Cannon-Bowers, J. A. & Salas, E. (eds.) (1998). *Making decisions under stress: Implications for individual and team training.* Washington DC: American Psychological Association.

Carter, A. J. & West, M. A. (1999). Sharing the burden – teamwork in health care settings. In J. Firth-Cozens & R. Payne (eds.), *Stress in health professionals* (pp. 191–202). Chichester, UK: Wiley.

Claxton, G. (1998a). *Hare brain tortoise mind – why intelligence increases when you think less.* London: Fourth Estate Ltd.

Claxton, G. L. (1998b). Knowing without knowing why: Investigating human intuition. *The Psychologist, 11*, 217–20.

Clouse, R. W. & Spurgeon, K. L. (1995). Corporate analysis of humor. *Psychology: A Journal of Human Behavior, 32*, 1–24.

Cohen, S. & Wills, T. A. (1985). Stress, social support, and the buffering hypothesis. *Psychological Bulletin, 98*, 310–57.

Cohen, S. G. & Bailey, D. E. (1997). What makes teams work? Group effectiveness research from the shop floor to the executive suite. *Journal of Management, 23*, 239–90.

De Dreu, C. K. W. & Van de Vliert, E. (eds.) (1997). *Using conflict in organizations.* London: Sage.

De Dreu, C. K. W. & Van Vianen, A. E. M. (2001). Responses to relationship conflict and team effectiveness. *Journal of Organizational Behavior, 22*, 309–28.

De Dreu, C. K. W. & West, M. A. (2001). Minority dissent and team innovation: The importance of participation in decision making. *Journal of Applied Psychology, 86*(6), 1191–201.

Deutsch, M. (1973). *The resolution of conflict: Constructive and destructive processes.* New Haven, CT: Yale University Press.

Devine, D. J. & Phillips, J. L. (2000). *Do smarter teams do better? A meta-analysis of team-level cognitive ability and team performance.* Presented at the 15th Annual Conference of the Society for Industrial-Organizational Psychology. April, New Orleans, LA.

Diehl, M. & Stroebe, W. (1987). Productivity loss in brainstorming groups: Towards the solution of a riddle, *Journal of Personality and Social Psychology, 53*, 497–509.

Dunbar, K. (1997). How scientists think: On-line creativity and conceptual change in science. In T. B. Ward, S. M. Smith, & J. Vaid (eds.), *Creative thought: An investigation of conceptual structures and processes* (pp. 461–93). Washington, DC: American Psychological Association.

Eagly, A. H. & Johnson, B. T. (1990). Leader and leadership style: A meta-analysis. *Journal of Applied Psychology, 108*, 233–56.

Earley, P. C. (1993). East meets West meets Mid East: further explorations of collectivistic and individualistic work groups. *Academy of Management Journal, 36*, 319–48.

Edelmann, R. (1993). *Interpersonal conflicts at work*. Leicester, UK: British Psychological Society.

Edmondson, A. C. (1996). Learning from mistakes is easier said than done: Group and organizational influences on the detection and correction of human error. *Journal of Applied Behavioral Science, 32,* 5–28.

Edmondson, A. C. (1999). Psychological safety and learning behavior in work teams. *Administrative Science Quarterly, 44,* 350–83.

Egan, G. (1986). *The skilled helper* (3rd edn). Pacific Grove, CA: Brooks Cole.

Fisher, R., Ury, W., & Patton, B. (1999). *Getting to yes: Negotiating an agreement without giving in*. London: Random House.

Flood, P., MacCurtain, S., & West, M. A. (2001). *Effective top management teams*. Dublin: Blackhall Press.

Fontana, D. (1989). *Managing stress*. Oxford: Blackwell.

Ford, C. M. & Gioia, D. A. (eds.) (1995). *Creative action in organizations: Ivory tower visions and real world voices*. London: Sage Publications.

Frone, M. R. (2000). Work–family conflict and employee psychiatric disorders: The national comorbidity survey. *Journal of Applied Psychology, 85,* 417–38.

Furnham, A., Steele, H., & Pendleton, D. (1993). A psychometric assessment of the Belbin team-role self-perception inventory. *Journal of Occupational and Organizational Psychology, 66,* 245–57.

Ganster, D. C., Fusilier, M. R., & Mayes, B. T. (1986). Role of social support in the experience of stress at work. *Journal of Applied Psychology, 71,* 102–10.

Gersick, C. J. G. (1988). Time and transitions in work teams: Toward a new model of group development. *Academy of Management Journal, 31,* 9–41.

Gersick, C. J. G. (1989). Marking time: Predictable transitions in work groups. *Academy of Management Journal, 32,* 274–309.

Goleman, D. (1995). *Emotional intelligence: Why it can matter more than IQ*. London: Bloomsbury.

Goleman, D. (2002). *The new leaders: Emotional intelligence at work*. London: Little, Brown.

Goleman, D., Boyatzis, R., & McKee, A. (2002). *The new leaders: Transforming the art of leadership into the science of results*. London: Little, Brown.

Gollwitzer, P. M. & J. A. Bargh (eds.) (1996). *The psychology of action: linking cognition and motivation to behavior*. New York: The Guilford Press.

Graen, G. & Scandura, T. A. (1987). Toward a psychology of dyadic organizing. *Research in Organizational Behavior, 9,* 175–208.

Guzzo, R. A. (1996). Fundamental considerations about work groups. In M. A. West (ed.), *The Handbook of Work Group Psychology* (pp. 3–23). Chichester, UK: John Wiley.

Guzzo, R. A. & Salas, E. (eds.) (1995). *Team effectiveness and decision-making in organizations*. San Francisco: Jossey-Bass.

Guzzo, R. A. & Shea, G. P. (1992). Group performance and intergroup relations. In M. D. Dunnette and L. M. Hough (eds.), *Handbook of industrial and organizational psychology* (2nd edn, pp. 269–313). Palo Alto, CA: Consulting Psychologists Press.

Hackman, J. R. (ed.) (1990). *Groups that work (and those that don't): Conditions for effective teamwork.* San Francisco: Jossey Bass.

Hackman, J. R. (2002). *Leading teams: Setting the stage for great performances.* Cambridge, MA: Harvard Business School Press.

Hackman, J. R. & Morris, C. G. (1975). Group tasks, group interaction processes, and group performance effectiveness: A review and proposed integration. In L. Berkowitz (ed.), *Advances in experimental social psychology* (Vol. 8, pp. 45–99). New York: Academic Press.

Hackman, J. R. & Oldham, G. R. (1976). Motivation through the design of work: Test of a theory. *Organizational Behavior and Human Performance, 16,* 250–79.

Harris, C. & Beyerlein, M. M. (2003). Team-based organization: Creating an environment for team success. In M. A. West, D. Tjosvold, & K. G. Smith (eds.), *Handbook of organizational teamwork and cooperative working* (pp. 187–210). Chichester, UK: Wiley.

Heller, F., Pusić, E., Strauss, G., & Wilpert, B. (1998). *Organizational participation: Myth and reality.* Oxford: Oxford University Press.

Henry, J. (2001). *Creativity management.* London: Sage.

Hewstone, M., Rubin, M., & Willis, H. (2002). Intergroup bias. *Annual Reviews of Psychology, 53,* 575–604.

Hill, M. (1982). Group versus individual performance. Are N + 1 heads better than one? *Psychological Bulletin, 91,* 517–31.

House, R. J. & Mitchell, T. R. (1974). A path goal theory of leadership. *Journal of Contemporary Business, 5,* 81–94.

Howell, J. & Avolio, B. (1993). Transformational leadership, transactional leadership, locus of control and support for innovation: Key predictors of consolidated business unit performance. *Journal of Applied Psychology, 78,* 891–902.

Ingham, A. G., Levinger, G., Graves, J., & Peckham, V. (1974). The Ringelmann effect: Studies of group size and group performance. *Journal of Experimental Social Psychology, 10,* 371–84.

Jackson, S. E. (1996). The consequences of diversity in multidisciplinary work teams. In M. A. West (ed.), *Handbook of work group psychology* (pp. 53–75). Chichester, UK: Wiley.

Janis, I. L. (1982). *Victims of groupthink.* Boston MA: Houghton Mifflin.

Jehn, K. (1997). A qualitative analysis of conflict types and dimensions in organizational groups. *Administrative Science Quarterly, 42,* 530–57.

Joshi, A. & Jackson, S. E. (2003). Managing workforce diversity to enhance cooperation in organizations. In M. A. West, D. Tjosvold, & K. G. Smith (eds.), *International handbook of organizational teamwork and cooperative working* (pp. 277–96). Chichester, UK: Wiley.

Kanter, R. M. (1983). *The change masters.* New York: Simon and Schuster.

Karau, S. J. & Williams, K. D. (1993). Social loafing: A meta-analytic review and theoretical integration. *Journal of Personality and Social Psychology, 65,* 681–706.

Korsgaard, M. A., Brodt, S. E., & Sapienza, H. J. (2003). Trust, identity, and attachment: Promoting individuals' cooperation in groups. In M. A. West,

D. Tjosvold, & K. G. Smith (eds.), *International handbook of organizational teamwork and cooperative working* (pp. 113–30). Chichester, UK: Wiley.

Koslowski, S. W. J. & Bell, B. S. (2002). Work groups and teams in organizations. In W. C. Borman, D. R. Ilgen, & R. J. Klimoski (eds.), *Comprehensive handbook of psychology (Vol. 12): Industrial and organizational psychology* (pp. 333–75). New York: Wiley.

Kravitz, D. A. & Martin, B. (1986). Ringelmann rediscovered: The original article. *Journal of Personality and Social Psychology, 67,* 35–47.

Lam, S. S. K. & Schaubroeck, J. (2000). Improving group decisions by better pooling of information: A comparative advantage of group decision support systems. *Journal of Applied Psychology, 85,* 565–73.

Latané, B. & Darley, J. M. (1970). *The unresponsive bystander: Why doesn't he help?* Englewood Cliffs, NJ: Prentice Hall.

Latané, B., Williams, K., & Harkins, S. (1979). Many hands make light the work: The causes and consequences of social loafing. *Journal of Personality and Social Psychology, 37,* 822–32.

Latham, G. P. & Locke, E. A. (1991). Self-regulation through goal setting. *Organizational Behavior and Human Decision Processes, 50,* 212–47.

Latham, G. P. & Yukl, G. A. (1975). A review of research on the application of goal setting in organizations. *Academy of Management Journal, 18,* 824–45.

Latham, G. P. & Yukl, G. A. (1976). Effects of assigned and participative goal setting on performance and job satisfaction. *Journal of Applied Psychology, 61,* 824–45.

Lauderdale, P., Smith-Cunnien, P., Parker, J., & Inverarity, J. (1984). External threat and the definition of deviance. *Journal of Personality and Social Psychology, 46,* 1058–68.

Leung, K., Lu, L., & Liang, X. (2003). When East meets West: Effective teamwork across cultures. In M. A. West, D. Tjosvold, & K. G. Smith (eds.), *International handbook of organizational teamwork and cooperative working* (pp. 551–72). Chichester, UK: Wiley.

Lewin, K. (1951). *Field theory in social science: Selected theoretical papers,* D. Cartwright (ed.). New York: Harper & Row.

Locke, E. (1990). The motivation sequence, the motivation hub, and the motivation core. *Organizational Behavior and Human Decision Making Processes, 50,* 288–99.

Locke, E. & Latham, G. (1991). *A theory of goal setting and task motivation.* Englewood Cliffs, NJ: Prentice-Hall.

Locke, E. A., Shaw, K. N., Saari, L. M., & Latham, G. P. (1981). Goal setting and task performance. *Psychological Bulletin, 90,* 125–52.

Macy, B. A. & Izumi, H. (1993). Organizational change, design and work innovation: A meta-analysis of 131 North American field studies – 1961–1991. *Research in Organizational Change and Development, 7,* 235–313.

Maier, N. R. F. & Solem, A. R. (1962). Improving solutions by turning choice situations into problems. *Personnel Psychology, 15,* 151–7.

Manning, M. R., Jackson, C. N., & Fusilier, M. R. (1996). Occupational stress, social support and the cost of healthcare. *Academy of Management Journal, 39*, 750–83.

March, J. G. (1994). *A primer on decision making*. New York: Free Press.

Marmot, M., Siegrist, J., Theorell, T., & Feeney, A. (1999). Health and the psychosocial environment at work. In: M. Marmot and R. G. Wilkinson (eds.), *Social determinants of health* (pp. 105–31). Oxford: Oxford Univesity Press.

Maznevski, M. L. (1994). Understanding our differences: Performance in decision making groups with diverse members. *Human Relations, 47*, 531–52.

McDaniel, M. A., Morgeson, F. P., Finnegan, E. B., Campion, M. A. & Braverman, E. P. (2001). Use of situational judgment tests to predict job performance: A clarification of the literature. *Journal of Applied Psychology 86*, 730–40.

McGrath, J. E. (1984). *Groups: Interaction and performance*. New York: Prentice Hall.

Milgram, S. (1963). Behavioral study of obedience. *Journal of Abnormal and Social Psychology, 67*, 371–8.

Milgram, S. (1965). Some conditions of obedience and disobedience to authority. *Human Relations, 18*, 57–76.

Milgram, S. (1974). *Obedience to authority*. New York: Harper and Row.

Mohrman, S., Cohen, S. & Mohrman, L. (1995). *Designing team based organizations*. London: Jossey Bass.

Moscovici, S. (1976). *Social influence and social change*. London: Academic Press.

Moscovici, S., Lage, E., & Naffrechoux, M. (1969). Influence of a consistent minority on the responses of a majority in a color perception task. *Sociometry, 32*, 365–80.

Moscovici, S., Mugny, G., & van Avermaet, E. (eds.) (1985). *Perspectives on minority influence*. Cambridge, UK: Cambridge University Press.

Mount, M. K., Barrick, M. R., & Stewart, G. L. (1998). Five-factor model of personality and performance in jobs involving interpersonal interactions. *Human Performance, 11*, 145–65.

Mullen, B. & Copper, C. (1994). The relation between group cohesiveness and performance: An integration. *Psychological Bulletin, 115*, 210–27.

Mumford, M. D. & Gustafson, S. B. (1988). Creativity syndrome: Integration, application and innovation. *Psychological Bulletin, 103*, 27–43.

Murphy, K. R. & Cleveland, J. N. (1995). *Understanding performance appraisal: Social, organizational and goal-based perspectives*. London: Sage.

Myers, A. P. & Briggs, I. B. (1962) *The Myers–Briggs type indicator*. San Diego, CA: Educational Testing Services.

Nemeth, C. J. (1989). The stimulating properties of dissent: The case of recall. Paper presented at the Third International Conference on Minority Influence, Perugia, Italy, June 22–24.

Nemeth, C. J. & Nemeth-Brown, B. (2003). Better than individuals? The potential benefits of dissent and diversity for group creativity. In P. Paulus

& B. Nijstad (eds.), *Group creativity* (pp. 66–84). Oxford: Oxford University Press.

Nemeth, C. J. & Owens, P. (1996). Making work groups more effective: The value of minority dissent. In M. A. West (ed.), *Handbook of work group psychology* (pp. 125–42). Chichester, UK: John Wiley.

Nemeth, C., Connell, J., Rogers, J., & Brown, K. (2001). Improving decision making by means of dissent. *Journal of Applied Social Psychology, 31,* 707–20.

Nemeth, C., Rogers, J., & Brown, K. (2001). Devil's advocate vs. authentic dissent: Stimulating quantity and quality. *European Journal of Social Psychology, 31,* 707–20.

Nicholson, N. (2000). *Managing the human animal.* London: Texere.

Nicholson, N. & West, M. A. (1988). *Managerial job change: Men and women in transition.* Cambridge, UK: Cambridge University Press.

Nisbett, R. E., Peng, K., Choi, I., & Norenzayan, A. (2001). Culture and systems of thought: Holistic vs. analytic cognition. *Psychological Review, 108,* 291–310.

Oldham, G. R. & Cummings, A. (1996). Employee creativity: Personal and contextual factors at work. *Academy of Management Journal, 39,* 607–34.

Parker, G., McAdams, J., & Zielinski, D. (2000). *Rewarding teams: Lessons from the trenches.* San Francisco, CA: Jossey Bass.

Parry, G. (1990). *Coping with crises.* Oxford: Blackwell.

Paulus, P. B. (2000). Groups, teams and creativity: The creative potential of idea-generating groups. *Applied Psychology: An International Review, 49,* 237–62.

Peterson, N. G., Mumford, M. D., Borman, W. C., et al. (2001). Understanding work using the occupational information network (ONET): Implications for practice and research. *Personnel Psychology, 54,* 451–92.

Peterson, R. L. (1997). A directive leadership style can be both virtue and vice: Evidence from elite and experimental groups. *Journal of Personality and Social Psychology, 72,* 1107–21.

Pinto, J. K. & Prescott, J. E. (1987). Changes in critical success factor importance over the life of a project. *Proceedings of Academy of Management* conference, New Orleans, 328–32.

Pondy, L. (1967). Organizational conflict: Concepts and models. *Administrative Science Quarterly, 17,* 296–320.

Poulton, B. C. & West, M. A. (1994). Primary health care team effectiveness: Developing a constituency approach. *Health and Social Care, 2,* 77–84.

Pritchard, R. D., Jones, S. D., Roth, P. L., Stuebing, K. K., & Ekeberg, S. E. (1988). Effects of group feedback, goal setting, and incentives on organizational productivity. *Journal of Applied Psychology, 73,* 337–58.

Rogelberg, S. G., Barnes-Farrell, J. L., & Lowe, C. A. (1992). The stepladder technique: An alternative group structure facilitating effective group decision-making. *Journal of Applied Psychology, 77,* 730–7.

Romanov, K., Appelberg, K., Honkasalo, M., & Koskenvuo, M. (1996). Recent interpersonal conflict at work and psychiatric morbidity: A prospective study of 15,530 employees aged 24–64. *Journal of Psychosomatic Research, 40,* 169–76.

Runco, M. A. & Pritzker, S. R. (1999a). *Encyclopaedia of creativity, Vol. 1, A-H.* London: Academic Press.

Runco, M. A. & Pritzker, S. R. (1999b). *Encyclopaedia of creativity, Vol. 2, I-Z.* London: Academic Press.

Rutte, C. G. (2003). Social loafing in teams. In M. A. West, D. Tjosvold, & K. G. Smith (eds.), *International handbook of organizational teamwork and cooperative working* (pp. 361–78). Chichester, UK: Wiley.

Schmidt, F. L. & Hunter, J. E. (1998). The validity and utility of selection methods in personnel psychology: Practical and theoretical implications of 85 years of research findings. *Psychological Bulletin, 124,* 262–74.

Schneider, B., Goldstein, H. W., & Smith, D. B. (1995). The ASA framework: An update. *Personnel Psychology, 48,* 747–74.

Schutz, W. C. (1967). *JOY: Expanding human awareness.* New York: Grove Press.

Seligman, M. E. P. (1998). *Learned optimism: How to change your mind and your life.* London: Pocket Books.

Semin, G. & Glendon, A. I. (1973). Polarization and the established group. *British Journal of Social and Clinical Psychology, 12,* 113–21.

Shaw, M. E. (1932). A comparison of individuals and small groups in the rational solution of complex problems. *American Journal of Psychology, 44,* 491–504.

Sherif, M., Harvey, O. J., White, B. J., Hood, W. R., & Sherif, C. W. (1961). *Intergroup conflict and co-operation: The Robber's Cave experiment.* Norman, OK: Institute of Group Relations.

Shore, L. M. & Barksdale, K. (1998). Examining degree of balance and level of obligation in the employment relationship: A social exchange approach. *Journal of Organizational Behavior, 19,* 731–44.

Slavin, R. E. (1983). When does cooperative learning increase student achievement? *Psychological Bulletin, 94,* 429–45.

Smith, P. B. & Bond, M. H. (1993). *Social psychology across cultures: Analysis and perspectives.* New York: Harvester Wheatsheaf.

Stasser, G. & Stewart, D. (1992). Discovery of hidden profiles by decision-making groups: Solving a problem versus making a judgment. *Journal of Personality and Social Psychology, 63,* 426–34.

Stein, A. A. (1976). Conflict and cohesion: A review of the literature. *Journal of Conflict Resolution, 20,* 143–72.

Steiner, I. D. (1972). *Group process and productivity.* New York: Academic Press.

Sternberg, R. J. (ed.) (2002). *Why smart people can be so stupid.* New Haven, CT: Yale University Press.

Sternberg, R. J. (2003). Responsibility: One of the other three Rs. *APA Monitor, 34,* 5.

Sternberg, R. J. & Lubart, T. I. (1996). Investing in creativity. *American Psychologist, 51,* 677–88.

Stevens, M. J. & Campion, M. A. (1994). The knowledge, skill, and ability requirements for teamwork: Implications for human resource management. *Journal of Management, 20,* 503–30.

Stevens, M. J. & Campion, M. A. (1999). Staffing work teams: Development and validation of a selection test for teamwork settings. *Journal of Management, 25*, 207–28.

Stroebe, W., Diehl, M., & Abakoumkin, G. (1996). Social compensation and the Köhler effect: Toward an explanation of motivation gains in group productivity. In E. H. Witte & J. H. Davis (eds.), *Understanding group behavior, vol. 2, Small group processes and interpersonal relations* (pp. 37–65). Mahwah, NJ: Lawrence Erlbaum.

Tajfel, H. (1970). Experiments in intergroup discrimination. *Scientific American, 223*, 96–102.

Tajfel, H. & Billig, M. (1974). Familiarity and categorization in intergroup behavior. *Journal of Experimental Social Psychology, 10*, 159–70.

Tannenbaum, S. I., Salas, E., & Cannon-Bowers, J. A. (1996) Promoting team effectiveness. In M. A. West (ed.), *Handbook of work group psychology* (pp. 503–29). Chichester, UK: Wiley.

Tjosvold, D. (1991). *Team organisation: An enduring competitive advantage.* Chichester, UK. John Wiley and Sons.

Tjosvold, D. (1998). Cooperative and competitive goal approaches to conflict: Accomplishments and challenges. *Applied Psychology: An International Review, 47*, 285–342.

Tubbs, M. E. (1986). Goal setting: A meta-analytic examination of the empirical evidence. *Journal of Applied Psychology, 71*, 474–83.

Tuckman, B. W. (1965). Developmental sequences in small groups. *Psychological Bulletin, 63*, 348–99.

Turner, J. C. (1985). Social categorization and the self-concept: A social cognitive theory of group behavior. In E. J. Lawler (ed.), *Advances in group processes: Theory and research* (vol. 2, pp. 77–122). Greenwich, CT: JAI Press.

Tziner, A. & Eden, D. (1985). Effects of crew composition on crew performance: Does the whole equal the sum of its parts? *Journal of Applied Psychology, 70*, 85–93.

Van Gundy, A. B. Jr. (1988). *Techniques of structured problem solving.* New York: Van Nostrand Reinhold.

Vinokur, A., Burnstein, E., Sechrest, L., & Wortman, P. M. (1985). Group decision making by experts: Field study of panels evaluating medical technologies. *Journal of Personality and Social Psychology, 49*, 70–84.

Walker, T. G. & Main, E. C. (1973). Choice shifts in political decision making: Federal judges and civil liberties cases. *Journal of Applied Social Psychology, 3*, 39–48.

Watson, W. E., Kumar, K., & Michaelsen, L. K. (1993). Cultural diversity's impact on interaction process and performance: Comparing homogeneous and diverse task groups. *Academy of Management Journal, 36*, 590–602.

Weick, K. E. (1995). *Sense making in organizations.* Thousand Oaks, CA: Sage.

Weldon, E. & Weingart, L. R. (1994). Group goals and group performance. *British Journal of Social Psychology, 32*, 307–34.

West, M. A. (ed.) (1996). *The handbook of work group psychology.* Chichester, UK: Wiley.

West, M. A. (1997). *Developing creativity in organizations*. Leicester, UK: British Psychological Society.

West, M. A. (2000). Reflexivity, revolution, and innovation in work teams. In M. M. Beyerlein, D. A. Johnson, & S. T. Beyerlein (eds.), *Product development teams* (pp. 1–29). Stamford, CT: JAI Press.

West, M. A. (2002). Sparkling fountains or stagnant ponds: An integrative model of creativity and innovation implementation in work groups. *Applied Psychology: An International Review, 51*, 355–87.

West, M. A. (2003). *The secrets of successful teams*. London: Duncan Baird.

West, M. A. & Anderson, N. R. (1996). Innovation in top management teams, *Journal of Applied Psychology, 81*, 680–93.

West, M. A. & Allen, N. A. (1997). Selecting for teamwork. In N. Anderson & P. Herriot (eds.), *International handbook of selection and assessment* (pp. 493–506). Chichester, UK: John Wiley & Sons.

West, M. A., Borrill, C., Dawson, J., et al. (2002). The link between the management of employees and patient mortality in acute hospitals. *The International Journal of Human Resource Management, 13*, (8), 1299–1310.

West, M. A., Borrill, C. S., & Unsworth, K. L. (1998). Team effectiveness in organizations. *International Review of Industrial and Organisational Psychology, 13*, 1–48.

West, M. A. & Farr, J. L. (1990). *Innovation and creativity at work: Psychological and organizational strategies*. Chichester, UK: John Wiley & Sons.

West, M. A. & Markiewicz, L. (2003). *Building team-based working. A practical guide to organizational transformation*. Oxford: Blackwell.

West, M. A., Patterson, M. G., & Dawson, J. (1999). A path to profit?: Teamwork at the top. *Centre Piece: The Magazine of Economic Performance, 4*(3), 7–11.

West, M. A., Tjosvold, D., & Smith, K. G. (eds.) (2003). *The international handbook of organizational teamwork and cooperative working*. Chichester, UK: Wiley.

Wiersema, M. F. & Bantel, K. A. (1992). Top management team demography and corporate strategic change. *Academy of Management Journal, 35*, 91–121.

Williams, J. G. and Solano, C. H. (1983). The social reality of feeling lonely: Friendship and reciprocation, *Personality and Social Psychology Bulletin, 9*, 237–42.

Williams, K. J. & Alliger, G. M. (1994). Role stressors, mood spillover, and perceptions of work–family conflict in employed parents. *Academy of Management Journal, 37*, 837–68.

Worchel, S., Lind, E. A., & Kaufman, K. H. (1975). Evaluations of group products as a function of expectations of group longevity, outcome of competition and publicity of evaluations. *Journal of Personality and Social Psychology, 31*, 1089–97.

Worchel, S., Rothgerber, H., Day, E. A., Hart, D., & Butemeyer, J. (1998). Social identity and individual productivity within groups. *British Journal of Social Psychology, 37*, 389–413.

Yukl, G. (1998). *Leadership in organizations* (4th edn.). London: Prentice Hall.

Author Index

Page references for figures are in italics

Subject Index